"[An] engaging memoir/style book . . . Burke's fans and anyone who has struggled with weight and attendant self-esteem issues will likely welcome the story of a once-slender, still beautiful woman who, rather than conform to an impossible (and possibly unhealthy) standard of body size, has chosen to celebrate what she is rather than to lament what she is not."
—*Publishers Weekly*

"Sexily plump, Delta is proof positive that a woman doesn't have to be slender to be a knockout. . . . Delta is a real role model for women who carry a few extra pounds."
—Liz Smith, *The New York Post*

"Burke unashamedly shares her views on life, makeup, and fashion . . . in a shoot-from-the-hip style. The result is fun reading"
—*Kirkus Review*

"[A] riveting account of her own rise to the top."
—*Globe*

"Why are we so unforgiving when it comes to 'real-size' actresses? If anyone is qualified to explain that paradox it's Burke."
—*The Atlanta Journal-Constitution*

W9-BTG-558

DELTA style

DELTA BURKE

with Alexis Lipsitz

ST. MARTIN'S GRIFFIN ♏ New York 🦁

DELTA *style*

Eve Wasn't a Size 6 and Neither Am I

DESIGN BY CAROL MALCOLM RUSSO / SIGNET M. DESIGN, INC.

DRAWINGS BY DELTA BURKE

Library of Congress Cataloging-in-Publication Data

Burke, Delta.
    Delta style : Eve wasn't a size 6 and neither am I / Delta Burke
with Alexis Lipsitz—1st ed.
        p.   cm.
    Includes bibliographical references.
    ISBN 0-312-19855-8
    1. Burke, Delta.   2. Actors—United States—Biography.   3.
Beauty, personal.   4. Overweight women—Costume.   I. Lipsitz,
Alexis.   II. Title.
PN2287.B793A3   1998
791.45'028'092—dc21
[B]   97-31523
                                                           CIP

First St. Martin's Griffin Edition: January 1999
10 9 8 7 6 5 4 3 2 1

In memory of

my wonderful Nana,

Ruby May Burton,

December 23, 1911—February 27, 1997,

and my loyal companion,

Blanche,

July 21, 1986—May 22, 1997,

together now in heaven

CONTENTS

I have a thing about crowns. The bigger, the better. I entered my first beauty pageant at the age of sixteen, and it wasn't long before I began catching on to the fact that some pageants have bigger crowns than others. Those were the ones I'd enter. At times I was even tempted to call up pageant officials and say, "I want to enter your pageant and how big is your crown?"

I still have two little pink carrying cases that were gifts to contestants at the Miss Orlando pageant of

1974. Inside one, wrapped in white tissue paper, are all of my crowns. Inside the other are the sashes that went with the crowns. There's Miss Flame, Miss Florida Flame, Miss All-America Girl, Miss Cover Girl, Miss Optimist of College Park, Miss All Veterans Day, Jamboree Queen, Orlando Action Princess, Miss Orlando, and Miss Florida. One I slept in. I even bought a couple myself, to replace the ones I thought weren't up to snuff.

My official Miss Florida crown. Orlando Sentinel. Ed Stout

Note the differences between my crown and my successor's. When it came time to give up my Miss Florida Flame crown, I didn't want to do it. So I bought myself a nice, new bigger one. Collection of Delta Burke

Some beauty queens are embarrassed to wear a crown in public, but not me. I'd show up at appearances in a chiffon gown, long white gloves, the robe, the scepter, the banner, the hair, the works—didn't matter whether I was opening a supermarket or riding a 400-pound hog at the state fair. It never

The quintessential beauty queen pose. Collection of Delta Burke

occurred to me how peculiar I may have looked. All I knew is that people treated me like a fairy princess, and I was a natural ham who loved the attention.

Crowns, like all things flashy and dramatic, were right up my alley. I thought they were a cure-all—I was always putting mine on some kid's head and expecting magical things to occur. But for me, crowns were also a means to an end, because I knew the direction I wanted to go. My ultimate goal was to be a famous actress and movie star, and my ticket out of town was pageants. Even when I was in the Miss America pageant, I had a fleeting thought that if I ran up and ripped the crown off the winner's head, I might get on *The Tonight Show*.

Today, when I rummage through those pink cases, the image that sticks in my mind is of a seventeen-year-old with a big crown on her head merrily zipping around town in a little car with a big sign saying DELTA BURKE, MISS FLORIDA emblazoned on the side—a seventeen-year-old who was skipping school to cut a ribbon or become an honorary Boy Scout or judge a nursing home pageant. What was going through the minds of the people who pulled up beside me as I turned to them and gave them my best pageant wave (open hand moving from side to side, not like that stuffy cupped wave the British royalty do— they could use a little more of that all-American "Hey, yah'll" kind of wave) and then burned rubber down the road?

And who knows what my classmates were thinking when, to avoid flunking out of high school, I went from classroom to classroom in an Anne Boleyn costume, on my knees doing a "Tomorrow I shall die" soliloquy in a Southern-twanged English accent? While everyone else was going on dates and cheering on the football team, I was showing up for a heart fund benefit in a belly dancer's costume and shimmying like a striptease artist. Who on earth was that person? And why was she doing these things?

I wanted to be a star, right from the get go. I have been in the public eye since I was fifteen, when I discovered acting. I

Among my more memorable experiences on the Miss Florida personal-appearance trail were my ride on a 400-pound hog named Nasty Ned and my afternoon with Shamu the whale. Top and bottom: © 1977 Sea World of Florida.

remember getting off the plane after my first acting job, which was playing nursery rhyme characters for Tupperware salesmen in a traveling Tupperware Jubilee. I made a beeline for my mother and said, "I know what I want to do the rest of my life." Meaning, of course, acting—not traveling around enter-

The costumes for my Anne Boleyn dramatic reading were designed by Mom and evolved as I climbed the Miss America pageant ladder.

Collection of Delta

taining Tupperware salesmen, although that in itself had its rewards. At the time, it was as big, glamorous, and exciting to me as anything I could imagine.

But being in the public eye for so long has also meant that I've had to do a lot of growing up in public over the years.

Even at fifteen, it occurred to me that I had an image to maintain. That kind of scrutiny doesn't afford you many goof-ups.

A head shot from my starlet days. Randee St. Nicholas

I learned that lesson too many times to count. It really hit home when I was nineteen and living in London, attending the London Academy of Music and Dramatic Arts (LAMDA); I was starving myself to lose weight and passed out down some stairs at a swanky dinner party. I learned it at twenty-one, when, all dewy-eyed and new in Hollywood, I carried a script to a Malibu party to show the bigwigs that I was a serious actress and discovered that I looked more like a juicy piece of prime rib—fresh meat—than an actress to them. I learned it

most painfully about five and a half years ago, when I was starring in the hit television show *Designing Women*. I had been
nominated for an Emmy two times. I was married to the love
of my life. But an unexpected thing happened. The press
attacked me because of what was perceived as a slipup in my
beauty queen image. I was gaining weight—and that weight
gain was very publicly chronicled because I was famous. I had
to stand in the grocery store checkout line next to tabloid
headlines that screamed I was devouring whole boxes of candy
and chasing people around on the set to get at their food. I had
to hear radio stations play songs like "Delta Dawn, How Much
Weight Have You Put On?"

I was totally unprepared for the constant invasions into my
private life. I became public property. Strangers felt they could
say anything to me. I remember one woman coming up to me
on the street in Massachusetts and pulling open my overcoat.
"Let's see, how big *are* you?" she said. Another time, I was
approached on a Natchez, Mississippi, corner by a woman who
blurted out, "You really *are* fat, aren't you?" Then there were
the constant allusions to my so-called pregnancy. People would
come up to me out of nowhere and ask, "When's the baby
due, Delta?" or "How far along are you?"

My mama raised me to be a lady, so for a long time I just
had to stand there and take it. I would answer, as sweetly as I
could, "No, I'm not pregnant, I'm just plain *fat.*" But after a
while, I couldn't help but react to the rudeness. "Hey!" I'd say,
gritting my teeth. "There's no baby in there, okay?"

Looking back, all the fuss seems silly. But at the time, it
really did hurt. I was struck not only by the ferocity of the
attacks but also because they contradicted my own feelings of
well-being. I had too long been a Hollywood trooper, doing
every interview and making every appearance and talking up
the latest project. For the first time in my life I had the nerve
to feel comfortable with my body—*my* body, not theirs. As I
grew more confident in my work and content in my personal

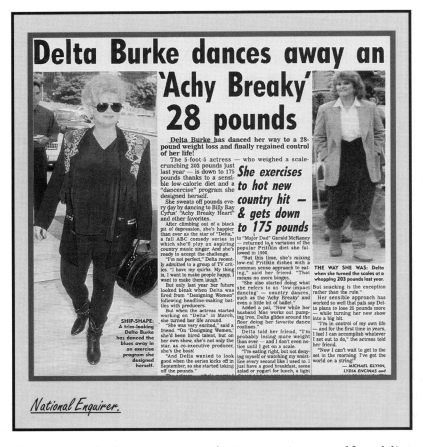

Delta Burke dances away an 'Achy Breaky' 28 pounds

Delta Burke has danced her way to a 28-pound weight loss and finally regained control of her life!

The 5-foot-5 actress — who weighed a scale-crunching 203 pounds just last year — is down to 175 pounds thanks to a sensible low-calorie diet and a "dancercise" program she designed herself.

She sweats off pounds every day by dancing to Billy Ray Cyrus' "Achy Breaky Heart" and other favorites.

After climbing out of a black pit of depression, she's happier than ever as the star of "Delta," a fall ABC comedy series in which she'll play an aspiring country music singer. And she's ready to accept the challenge.

"I'm not perfect," Delta recently admitted to a group of TV critics. "I have my quirks. My thing is, I want to make people happy, I want to make them laugh."

But only last year her future looked bleak when Delta was fired from "Designing Women" following headline-making battles with producers.

But when the actress started working on "Delta" in March, she turned her life around.

"She was very excited," said a friend. "On 'Designing Women,' she'd been hired talent, but on her own show, she's not only the star, as co-executive producer, she's the boss!

"And Delta wanted to look good when the series kicks off in September, so she started taking off the pounds."

She exercises to hot new country hit — & gets down to 175 pounds

to "Major Dad" Gerald McRaney — returned to a variation of the popular Pritikin diet she followed in 1990.

"But this time, she's mixing low-cal Pritikin dishes with a common sense approach to eating," said her friend. "That means no more binges.

"She also started doing what she refers to as 'low-impact dancing' — country dances, such as the 'Achy Breaky' and even a little bit of ballet."

Added a pal, "Now while her husband Mac works out pumping iron, Delta glides around the floor doing her favorite dance routines."

Delta told her friend, "I'm probably losing more weight than ever — and I don't even notice until I get on a scale.

"I'm eating right, but not denying myself or watching my waistline every second like I used to. I just have a good breakfast, some salad or yogurt for lunch, a light

THE WAY SHE WAS: Delta when she turned the scales at a whopping 203 pounds last year.

Her sensible approach has worked so well that pals say Delta plans to lose 25 pounds more — while turning her new show into a big hit.

"I'm in control of my own life — and for the first time in years, I feel I can accomplish whatever I set out to do," the actress told her friend.

"Now I can't wait to get to the set in the morning I've got the world on a string!"

— MICHAEL GLYNN, LYDIA ENCINAS and

SHIP-SHAPE: A trim-looking Delta Burke has danced the blues away in an exercise program she designed herself.

National Enquirer.

life, I stopped obsessing over calories, starving myself, and living on diet pills to look skinny for the cameras. You see, by nature I have never been a skinny girl. I have always had curves. As my mother will tell you, there is not a female member of our extended family who is under a size 12. We are a family of big, bosomy Southern girls, and we are proud of it.

But even as the full-figured real me emerged, I never stopped wanting to feel sexy, attractive, and loved. So I made adjustments. I had great-looking clothes made for me because the stores simply didn't offer many choices. I wore my hair a little bigger. But the tabloid barrage made self-esteem an impossible goal. As it continued I became less and less confident, until I finally withdrew completely. My whole body language changed—I dropped my head, I rounded my shoulders, I wore my hair in my face. I was made to feel shamed. I wouldn't even go out of the house for fear that some photographer would be lurking in the bushes to snap me by surprise.

With time, I got through it. But every day is still a bit of a fight. During the worst of the tabloid abuse I received a wonderful note from Elizabeth Taylor, thanking me for describing her as a role model and calling me "beautiful, courageous, and radiant." It was like a letter from God. I carried that letter around in my purse till it practically disintegrated in my hands.

But what meant the most to me were the thousands of letters of support from real-size women all over. Your letters made the difference—the nicest, warmest letters and phone calls you can imagine. These letters encouraged me to see the tabloid stories for what they were—petty sniping at an easy target—and helped me become stronger. Many of those letters I shoved straight into my purse, right next to Elizabeth Taylor's note. Those crumpled little pieces of paper were like diamonds to me. To those who wrote, who encouraged, who made me cry when I heard their own stories, I am overwhelmingly grateful. This book is for you.

I have been fortunate to work with people who are the best at what they do. Celebrated designers, costumers, hairstylists, and makeup artists have all taught me techniques I use to develop my own personal style. In *Delta Style,* I am passing along these tools and practical advice, to help all women, who in their search for personal growth are seeking out their own wonderful style. As I talk about different techniques, I'll share stories and events in my life that I hope demonstrate the power and strength that anyone can develop when she applies these tools to her own desires. It's all about learning to use simple, practical skills to realize personal empowerment—for body and soul.

It's amazing how a skinny piece of rhinestoned metal made this seventeen-year-old feel like a goddess. Jean Korb

These days, nothing's really changed about the things I like and the things I want. I still love being a ham and performing. I still love the crowns and the flashy tiaras. It's amazing how a flimsy piece of metal with rhinestones stuck on it can still make a shy, insecure little girl feel like a goddess. The difference now is that I feel I *deserve* to wear them. All my life I have been trying to please other people, working from the *outside in:* letting my appearance reflect what I thought people wanted me to be, hoping the message I sent would be the one they wanted to hear, trying to fit in by molding my looks to what I guessed was someone else's image of me. In the process of becoming more confident and sure of myself, I stopped trying to satisfy others' expectations. I stopped trying to fit into a mold that was never meant for me. Today, while I still love dressing up and flashy costumes, what's changed is that my appearance is truly a reflection of me. I'm operating from the *inside out.*

All women deserve to feel beautiful, confident, and true to who they are—not to some idealized image that is foisted upon us. The tools I'm passing along to you can open up a world of choices and give you the practical know-how to show off on the outside what you feel on the inside. No matter what size or shape or age or color you are, let *Delta Style* be a guide to finding and celebrating your own wonderful self— and rediscovering the goddess in you.

DELTA style

A Cat Named Delta

People always ask me about my name. After I was born, on a hot July 30, my mother asked my uncle Jimmy what I looked like—those being the days when the mother was the last person to see the new baby. There had been some whispering about a pointy head, but Jimmy, the jokester in the family, dismissed that. That baby's head is fine, he told Mother, but she has eyes like that cat you used to have, and she's pretty hairy, to boot. Just like Delta (the family cat!). After that, my mom couldn't get the name out of her head. Then, when she saw me, it stuck. Although I wasn't at all hairy, I had blue eyes. Just like Delta the cat.

Bewitched

Growing up in Florida fed my imagination. My mother was a Mississippi beauty, Gulfport's Miss Hospitality of 1951, whose own mother came from a family of seven sisters. My stepfather was movie-star handsome. Orlando, Florida, was quite a different place then. It had a slow-moving, small-town feel amid a lush, bigger-than-life landscape. Our yard was full of fantastical tropical plants, banana trees, and elephant ears. Pink and red hibiscus bloomed all over. The Florida sun never seemed to stop shining.

The house I grew up in sat in a dense forest of live oaks and pines at the edge of town. In one direction was town, in another, cows in a field, and all around me, sweet-smelling orange groves. The house was a farmhouse variation on a Cape Cod—style structure, a little unusual for Florida, where pastels and stucco were the norm. Like me, a little unusual for Florida. Needless to say, it was the only house for miles around that looked like that. An elderly lady had lived in it for years before us, and it was known to the neighborhood kids as the Witch's House. When I was young, my mother had very long hair, to her waist, and loved to do a witch cackle whenever children walked by the house—although she denies it to this day. When friends came to visit me, all they'd see would be a hand reaching out from behind the louvered door to close it, very slowly, very dramatically.

She swears up and down that she did that only at Halloween. Well, it seemed like I heard that witch cackle an awful lot. Every place we went, there always seemed to be a witch on the premises.

My mother was wonderful. We were always visiting nearby parks, where she'd tell me the name of every tree and animal and make up a little story about each one. She delighted in feeding my fantasies, and I had a pretty active fantasy life of my own. I was an only child for seven years, but I had no trouble

A vision in pink: my mother, Jean Burton, Gulfport's Miss Hospitality 1951. Collection of Delta Burke

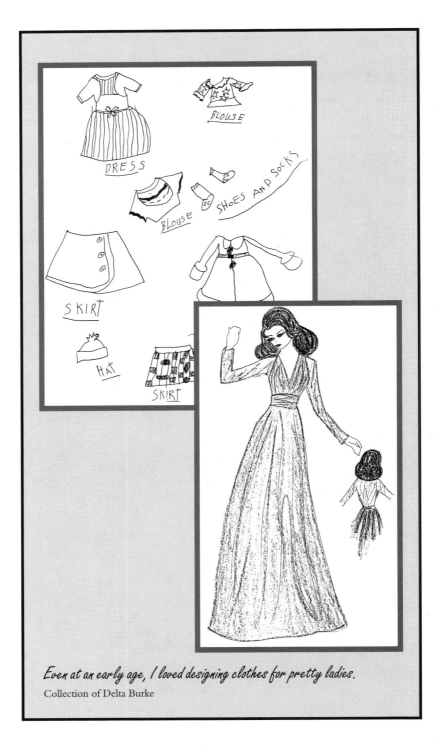

Even at an early age, I loved designing clothes for pretty ladies.
Collection of Delta Burke

amusing myself. I spent my days running barefoot in the woods, coming home with purple feet from climbing mulberry trees. My nights I spent in my attic bedroom, where I would happily draw and play-act for hours alone. Even then, I was big on drawing costumes and my pretty ladies.

Mother would come up with elaborate costumes for me and go to great lengths to make them appear authentic. In the fifth grade I played Queen Elizabeth I in a play. For the bodice, Mother covered an old long-line bra in brocade and velvet. She draped a choker necklace onto the bodice and pinned it there and then added rhinestone brooches. For the skirt, she used a real family heirloom, an 1830 tobacco-colored silk skirt. Gold paper from used cigarette boxes was used to make my cardboard crown. I still have that crown!

Because Mother made every event so magical, I clung to childhood rituals long after the other kids had given them up. At Christmas, Mother laid gifts out in the traditional way, under the tree—but then she'd strategically place presents in the fireplace, in the yard, as if they had accidentally dropped out of Santa's sack. We would leave cookies and milk for Santa (like all the other kids did). But then she would go that extra step and leave a bowl of sugar for the reindeer. And as I lay sleeping, she would nibble the cookies, sip the milk, have the dog lick the sugar bowl, and then place all of this on the roof outside my attic window, so that it looked like I had just missed the whole damn thing. At Easter she would make little bunny prints with her fingers in the sand and dirt all the way out the front yard. It still makes me smile, picturing my mother out in the dead of night on her knees making bunny prints.

The Blonde in the Classroom, Part I

The star in my first-grade classroom was a real pretty girl with long blond hair. The boys would make such a fuss over that girl! And I noticed they didn't fuss over me. I wasn't the pretty one.

5

Oh, I had lots of personality; I was cute and spunky, but I didn't *feel* like the pretty one, in that golden-blond All-American way. I was a Florida gal with dark hair and lily-white skin.

That was my initiation to the power of appearance and the message the way you look sends. Of course, I was to realize much later that if you don't develop yourself in other ways—if you're all sizzle and no steak—you end up a pretty hollow vessel that always tries, but never seems able, to fill up from the outside in. That's what I know now. For a long time, however, no matter how many crowns, all I wanted was to be that pretty blonde in the classroom.

I never really fit in at school. I had been an only child for so long that it made me a bit of a loner. I ran free in the woods

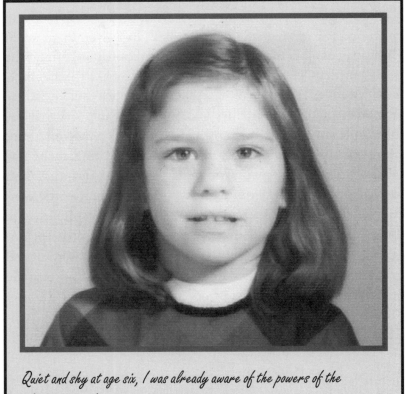

Quiet and shy at age six, I was already aware of the powers of the blonde in the classroom. Collection of Delta Burke

and spent hours playing by my grandmother's lake. I entertained myself by drawing, dancing, and play-acting in the attic. I found that creating characters and wearing costumes let me become someone far more dazzling than the girl I thought I was.

Because I was so shy, I was easy to bully and wasn't a good fighter. And sometimes that would come back to slap me in the face. I'll never forget one Halloween when the school gave out costumes to kids who wanted them. My mother usually made mine, so I didn't order one. When the costumes came in, I watched, thrilled and excited, as the kids pulled each costume out of the box. I was so happy for everyone; I clapped and laughed as each box was opened. Finally the teacher looked at me and snapped, "What are you so happy about? *You're* not getting one." With that, I pulled back and withdrew. I had been so excited: I knew the magic that comes from disappearing inside an exotic costume, becoming a character that was much more interesting than yourself.

The Transformation

As I mentioned, I was an only child and grandchild for seven years. I spent a lot of play time alone. Yet I felt much loved and cherished. Even the arrival of my brother, Jonathan, when I was seven, and sister, Jennifer, when I was ten, did little to diminish my sense of well-being within the family; there were just more people around to play with and love to death. You would have thought with all that attention I'd have developed strong self-esteem. But I didn't. I wasn't into sports, I didn't have any kind of outlet, I didn't really belong to any group. I had grown up with a rich interior life in that attic room. Out of my cozy family cocoon I was painfully shy. By the time I turned thirteen, Mother thought a course in modeling school might nudge me out of my shell and help me feel better about myself. She never pushed me—it was more of a gentle suggestion. With nothing to lose, I agreed.

Modeling school—and the fashion shows and beauty pageants that followed—opened up a whole new world for me. It helped me combat my shyness and allowed me to develop social skills. Truly, that's when I thought everything came together for me.

❝ *She just thought she was the ugliest thing in the world. At that time, I had the other two children, one a baby, one a toddler. So I would take Delta to classes and then go to a soda shop with the two little ones and wait for the class to be over. Me and the family—always driving Delta around in the car.* ❞

—Jean Burke, Delta's mother

One little modeling course created a monster. I was named to Montgomery Ward's Teen Board, where a select group of area kids modeled, served as Santa's helpers, and did general promotions for the store. At fifteen, I was "discovered" after I talked my way into a summer job with Tupperware, whose headquarters were in Kissimee, Florida. The company sponsored an annual road show, called the Tupperware Jubilee, where actors performed nursery rhyme skits for Tupperware salesmen. (I guess the sight of actors emoting Mother Goose tales was supposed to drive the salesmen into a Tupperware-selling frenzy.) Nevertheless, my first acting job—when I first got paid for acting—gave me an unforgettable taste of show business. And what a taste: Those Tupperware shows were huge conventions, sometimes even held in football stadiums. The audience participated in some of the skits for prizes, so there was a general atmosphere of mass hysteria. I threw myself heart and soul into portrayals of Mary Quite Contrary and Tinker Bell. I remember getting sick and having to go to the hospital and being unceremoniously stuffed into a car still wearing Mary Quite Contrary's wedding gown, with its giant hoop skirt. I can still see myself lying on a hospital table with that big old hoop sticking way up. No question, I was smitten with show biz. There was no turning back now.

❝ *I thought, How can I let my daughter go? You get all these reassurances from people: Oh, she'll be well taken care of. But of course I was a nervous wreck. And the first thing she said to me when she got off that plane was, 'I know exactly what I'm going to do the rest of my life. This is what I'm going to do, this is it.'* ❞
—Jean Burke

Dressed as Tinker Bell for the Tupperware Jubilee. P.S. I still have the wings and the wand! Collection of Delta Burke

The Pageant Consortium

I entered my first beauty pageant at sixteen. I had heard about it over the school intercom: The winner was to represent the local fire department and promote fire awareness. Miss Flame. It seemed like the next thing to do. I had, after all, taken all those modeling classes. I was determined not to lose the momentum and have all those feelings of self-confidence melt away. Mother and my grandmother Nana were my coaches, cheerleaders, and coconspirators. We were the perfect team, a real pageant consortium. The whole process became great sport for us girls. For my first appearance in the Miss Flame pageant, I wore a brown and white dress that was bought at an Orlando department store for $40. Paying $40 for a dress was a big deal; it made quite an impression on us. It must have made an impression on the judges as well, because I made it to the final competition. For that, I wore a dreamy tangerine chiffon gown—it was the big time. I felt light as a feather in that dress. And then I saw the contestant ahead of me appearing like an antebellum vision in a blue Scarlett O'Hara gown, with a giant hoop skirt and a cascade of ruffles. Oh, boy, I thought. That does it. I don't have a chance. I wanted a gown like *that*.

Fortunately, the judges were not swayed by regional pride—or that blue gown. Although I was a nervous wreck and acted on instinct alone, I won! My God, I thought, I may actually have a knack for this.

As Miss Flame, it was my proud duty to shimmy down firepoles for a year. After that, I won fifteen out of sixteen pageants I entered. (The one pageant I lost was the Tangerine Bowl Queen crown. I'm *still* irked about losing that crown.)

My pageant consortium was unbeatable. It became a family hobby, no different really from preparing for a swim meet. Even my father had an influence; he helped psych me up

Pageant blitz: I won Miss Orlando Flame and went on to win Miss Florida Flame; here I am, newly crowned, with my court. Collection of Delta Burke

before the contests with his infectious "can't lose" attitude. We spied on the competition; we snooped when the judges huddled together. Nana would trail behind me and pick up what people were saying as I passed, then report back to us so we could analyze what I was doing right and how to fix any flaws. During the Miss "All American Girl" pageant, the consortium learned the identity of the winner even before it was announced. Because I wore a big white chiffon gown in several pageants, I had become known in pageant circles as Snow White. In snooping around, my mother overheard the pageant scuttlebutt, which was that Snow White was the big winner.

People often ask me if I ever felt exploited or coerced into entering beauty pageants, and I have to say *no way*. For one thing, I got into pageants relatively late, at sixteen, and doing so was all my decision. Getting up on stage, being a ham,

I loved to dress up and pose for Mom in the backyard. Collection of Delta Burke

wearing crowns—I soon discovered all this was right up my alley. For another, I recognized early on that for me pageants were a means to an end, so in that sense I exploited the heck out of *them*. Emotionally, they filled me up; they gave me a sense of myself. Finally—a place I fit in! Pageants gave me my identity.

The pageants, the acting road shows, and the modeling all showcased a certain inbred flamboyance. I was always able to play a role. Outrageous costumes and exotic personalities allowed me to become someone else, which at that time made me more comfortable than being me. My theatrics were not limited to beauty contests. Oh, *no*. A typical day's school outfit might be hot pants and thigh-high vinyl boots—which everyone thought was a damned peculiar accessory in hothouse Florida. At sixteen I remember being politely told that my services would not be needed for a school talent show—my outfit and dance were regarded as a little too risqué. (My act consisted of going on stage in a belly-dancing costume and performing a personally choreographed bump-and-grind to the song "War!")

I may have been shy, but another part of me just went about my merry, flamboyant way, blissfully ignorant of the irony of it. I wasn't interested in real life, and it didn't seem interested in me. We kind of went our own ways. I wanted to be a star. Because my own sense of self was so shaky, dressing up let me become someone more beautiful, poised, and outgoing than I thought I was. It was odd, my wearing sexy costumes to beat the band and entering beauty pageants—yet having little social life and being uncomfortable with my looks and the reactions I got. Granted, I was clueless, but I didn't think the reason for that naïveté was anything more than being shy and sheltered.

All that freedom from the real world changed dramatically at sixteen, when, happily rolling an inner tube down the dirt road leading from my grandmother's house, I got a terrible feeling. The road had always been seen in my mind as the way to the Scary Place, for reasons long forgotten. Only now I remembered why. The memories came trickling in, in bits and pieces—how I had traveled down that same path when I was only four years old, going to visit my friend, and how her teenage brother had "played" with me, and how uncomfortable it made me feel. I remembered going to my mother—and she *listened* to me. She never scoffed or laughed or accused me of lying. Other things came back to me: the bright lights of the doctor's office, the gloves, and Momma going to their house. And suddenly it occurred to me that it was from that point on that my friend and I were never quite friends again.

I ran home, inner tube and all, and went to my grandmother and asked her if I had dreamed it all. Had my neighbor's brother actually molested me? She looked at me for a long time and then said yes.

I don't want to make too much of this—the fact that my mother listened to me probably helped me avoid major problems later on. But the molestation did have a profound effect on me for a long time. Now I understood why I couldn't deal with people's sexual interest in me. It made me uncomfortable; it scared and frightened me. At times I think I gained weight because it felt safer to be heavier. I could hide behind the weight and be invisible. When I'd get thin, I would have to deal with sexual power again, and I was poorly equipped to do so.

In truth, I think that few of us are prepared to deal with our sexual power when we are teenagers and young women. It was something I would wrestle with for many years.

Beauty Pageant Blitz

I discovered I was good at pageants. In one year, I won ten of eleven contests, a feat one local newspaper described as a "blitz on the beauty contest circuit." Interviews became commonplace and forced me to talk about myself, helping me overcome my natural shyness. I was a popular interview subject, because I tended to be slightly offbeat and a bit more forthright than most other pageant winners. It was all new territory for me, but I could gab with the best of them. "If I ever get to the Miss America pageant," I proclaimed to a *Miami Herald* reporter, "I just want to make the top ten and be able to show my acting

Here I am putting my first Anne Boleyn costume to good use—wearing it in the Central Florida Civic Theatre production of The Innocents.

Civic Theatre of Central Florida, Orlando. Jack Dunathan

talent on TV, knowing that millions of people are watching. It could help my career." It made perfect sense to me.

While all this was going on, I had no "normal" high school life. All I did was work as a model, go to acting classes, and enter beauty pageants. I started doing Central Florida Civic Theatre productions like *House of Blue Leaves, The Innocents,* and *Aladdin*—at fifteen. (I did Blanche du Bois in *A Streetcar Named Desire* at the Civic Theatre when I was nineteen, and I was a damned fabulous Blanche, if I do say so myself. *It's in the bones.* I got great reviews, although one reviewer said I sounded like Flip Wilson whenever I said "honey.")

I didn't have time for the usual high school things. My schoolmates just thought I was stuck-up. I had stopped dating, because I thought guys were so demanding. I had to convince myself that I didn't miss it, for I was involved in my "career." Oh, yes, I did have to have one date, just so people would leave me alone. In a picture I kept of that date, I'm wearing a wig the size of a small Volkswagen, the beginning of Big Hair.

I was definitely living on another planet.

The Miss Orlando pageant was a big step up. Talent counted for half the points in the judging, so my mother and I researched and wrote a part of a soliloquy recounting Anne Boleyn's final hours in the Tower of London before her beheading. The talent presentation had to be three minutes or less, which was tough to do with drama, but we were able to whittle a ten-minute speech down to a lean, mean two minutes and fifty-five seconds. It starts out with Anne Boleyn in the Tower of London, praying to God.

I can't believe that in a few moments, I shall be dead! I'm the queen! The queen of England! Henry gave up his wife of twenty years for me. He fought the pope for six and then made England Protestant, so he could marry me—ME! And now—he wants—my head.

Yesterday I saw my dear brother and four other innocent young men—beheaded! All because of me. They made me watch it. And the blood—Oh, God—the blood was everywhere!

My dear Lord—you who can look into my very soul know that I am innocent! But if it is your will that I must die here today—Oh dear merciful God!—please, please give me the strength and the courage to die like a queen. I was never accepted as queen. Please, God, at least let me die like one! Oh God—I'm so terribly afraid to die! Stay with me, Father.

[Drums roll. Anne Boleyn rises, crosses the stage to the scaffold, where she addresses the public, who are there to witness the execution.]

Good Christian people, I am come hither to die. For according to the law, and by the law, I am judged to die. And thus—I take my leave of the world, and of you all. And let it be said—she died like a queen.

To Christ, I commend my soul—sweet Jesus, receive my soul.

I am ready, Father.

It was a big hit. I cried when I performed it.

❝ **Her reading of Anne Boleyn's speech in the infamous Tower of London prison before her execution brought a hush over the crowd gathered in the cold and drizzling rain at the Eola bandshell.❞** —*Orlando Sentinel, 1973*

I won. I was Miss Orlando 1974. I went home with an official Miss America pageant crown, which I slept in. Before I went to sleep, I counted all the rhinestones; I believe there were five hundred. I was seventeen and overly excitable. I took my first step down that yellow brick road stretching out before me.

How to Skip Classes and Graduate High School

I had just won Miss Orlando, but I wasn't doing so hot in certain classes—school not really being my forte, you know. I had the smarts, but I was always skipping school to go cut a ribbon somewhere. Mother would send notes so outlandish the teachers would put them up on the bulletin board: notes that I had been held hostage, or that a devastating disease had befallen the family, "and Delta must stay at home today to nurse the family back to health!" My mother had a flair for the dramatic.

> Dear Miss—
> Please excuse Delta's absence from school yesterday. She was kidnapped by someone who looked exactly like the Mayor! Fortunately, she managed to cut her ribbon and escape —
> Sincerely —
> Mrs F. C. Burke—

A typical note from my mother to school excusing my absence.

Collection of Delta Burke

And then there I would be on the front page of the next morning's newspaper, in full pageant regalia for all to see, snipping away at a ribbon or opening up a new mall. What were we thinking? The teachers would roll their eyes and say, "Oh, yeah, *devastating* disease, Delta."

But once I won Miss Orlando, the faculty of Colonial High realized this pageant stuff was a serious thing with me and let me get away with missing classes and tests. I guess it

Graduate, Colonial High School, 1974. Collection of Delta Burke

brought some glory to the old school. Still, something had to give. I had to show some sort of scholastic aptitude to pass my classes and graduate. So my dear drama teacher, Miss Patricia Jenkins, went around to the classes I was failing and said, "Now, you know that Delta can't compete in the Miss Florida pageant if she doesn't graduate. If she comes around and does her talent show for you, will you give her a passing grade?" And, believe it or not, they all said yes. I think I spent two days in my Anne Boleyn costume, going from class to class—six performances a day—doing Anne Boleyn with the kids sitting *this* close to me. I would be falling down on my knees, crying out, "I can't believe that in a few more moments I shall be dead!" and weeping, all while the kids were muttering, "What the heck is she doing?"

P.S. I graduated.

The Crown That Got Away

My pageant success had made an impression on my school-mates after all. In my senior year I was voted Most Likely to Succeed. The standoffish—or so I imagined—cheerleaders, who had never in the past paid much attention to me, even showed up at the pageant to do a yell! I was impressed and very flattered.

Both Mom and I felt that my young age might work against me in the Miss Florida pageant of 1974. After all, many of the contestants were in their twenties and had been in the pageant loop since their teens. The Florida newspapers picked up on the youth versus experience theme: Would a seventeen-year-old rel-ative novice sweep the seasoned twenty-four-year-olds?

I think that's why I was so relaxed about it all: no expecta-tions. I did my Tower of London speech without a hitch and won the talent competition. I also swept the swimsuit competi-tion: I had gotten my dress size to a nerve-rattling 8, but my

My name is called as Miss Florida 1974. Collection of Delta Burke

proportions, at 35-23-36, stayed curvy. Lucky for me, curves were in that year.

On pageant day, my mother sent me a final note, saying POINT ONE IN EACH DIRECTION—meaning stand up straight and stick your chest out, girl! Still, when I heard my name announced as the winner, I clasped my hands to my face and let out a yelp. Then I saw my mother and grandmother and really started crying. It was the pageant consortium's finest hour.

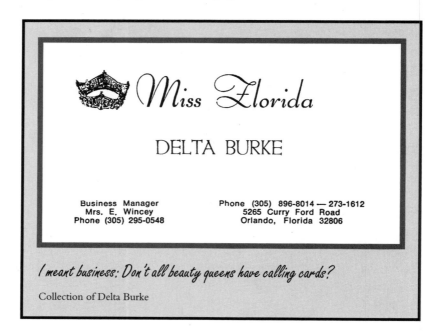

Miss Florida

DELTA BURKE

Business Manager
Mrs. E. Wincey
Phone (305) 295-0548

Phone (305) 896-8014 — 273-1612
5265 Curry Ford Road
Orlando, Florida 32806

I meant business: Don't all beauty queens have calling cards?

Collection of Delta Burke

At seventeen, I was the youngest Miss Florida ever, and perhaps the most naive. I mean, I was shocked to see girls there smoking. *How scandalous.* But in postpageant press articles I sounded like a seasoned veteran. The pageant was only the "beginning of phase three of her Atlantic City juggernaut," one article reported. "Hard-Driving Delta Set On Acting Career" blared another headline.

I returned home, victorious, wearing my official Miss America state crown. As Miss Florida, I won the use of a new

Ingenue on the loose! As Miss Florida, I traveled to the Plaza Hotel in New York, where a photographer snapped me as the fancy-free New Girl in Town. Jack Smith

Toyota for a year, to drive to official functions and the like. I wasn't so crazy about the car they offered me, so I went down to the Toyota dealership and talked them into giving me a nicer one—in exchange for appearances, commercials, and photo opportunities. It was mine for the year that I would reign, replacing a 1966 Chevrolet that classmates nicknamed "Burke's Bomb Bessie."

Aside from driving my new Toyota, I spent the summer preparing for the Miss America pageant. I met with state pageant judges to discuss where my strengths and weaknesses were. (In places like Texas, they start preparing you right out of the cradle.) The pageant handlers decided I should get a tan and lose some weight. The tan I wasn't going for, because I recognized that my pale complexion and black hair was the look that worked for me. But of course, they knew more about my body than I did, so to lose weight, I turned to water pills, diuretics. The weight would come right off, but so would the good stuff, like vitamins and minerals. I was definitely messing with my metabolism.

There are other insider beauty pageant tricks one learns along the way. In the Miss America pageant, hairpieces, false eyelashes, even falsies are allowed. I guess they figure in a pageant where talent and personal interviews count so much, you might need a little help with the other stuff. One of my favorite tricks? Smearing Vaseline on my teeth. No, this is not to make the teeth shine; you do it to keep your lips from getting stuck way up above the teeth, a side effect of smiling for hours on end.

So, armed with my hairpieces, my false lashes, and my petroleum jelly, I traveled to Atlantic City less than three months after winning Miss Florida. My twelve pieces of luggage looked like toys compared with the crates contestants from the more established pageants rolled in with, many containing $10,000 wardrobes. But that didn't faze me—I was on a winning streak. And I knew that by becoming Miss

America or at least breaking into the top ten, it would grease my way into the big time—show biz. I chirped merrily to the pageant judges that, oh no, I didn't care about the scholarship money. No, sir, I was going to be a star. And they just frowned upon that.

Indeed, I was the youngest contestant in the pageant. But it wasn't my age that affected the outcome in the Miss America pageant. No, I was doomed the minute I was paired with Miss Georgia for publicity events and photos. Miss Georgia was a very sweet person who happened to have the thickest Southern drawl I'd ever heard. My Florida drawl *paled* in comparison. By the time of the talent competition—me wearing my new and improved Anne Boleyn hat, basically a dyed black bridal hat with seed pearls glued onto it with Elmer's glue—my previously fail-safe Tower of London speech sounded something like, "Ah cain't buh-lieve that in a few mo' moments I shall be da-ud!"

It was much more than that, of course. I was more nervous than I had been in any other pageant. So I put on too much makeup and I did my hair up too big. For the swimsuit competition I even stuffed my brassiere. Well, everyone else was doing it. I grabbed a fistful of toilet paper and went to work. Again: too big. It made me bulge from every direction! I realized I had made a mistake while I was waiting in the wings, but my chaperone wouldn't let me run back and unstuff myself. So I was forced to walk the Atlantic City runway, a runway you could land a plane on, with my bosoms poking out to here, my hair standing up to here, and a lipstick-smeared grin plastered on my face.

Even so, I was devastated when I didn't make top ten in the 1974 Miss America pageant. When you're used to winning—I had, after all, won twelve or thirteen out of nineteen pageants entered—it was hard to lose the big one. Plus that crown was a doozy. Interestingly enough, I did get to wear the crown later, when former Miss America Mary Ann Mobley made a guest

Me being crowned by Mary Ann Mobley. She is the standard to which all Southern beauty queen belles aspire! Collection of Delta Burke appearance on *Designing Women*. I begged Mary Ann to bring it to the set, where I plopped it on my head and kept it there most of the week. At last: The official Miss America pageant crown was mine.

It wasn't a total loss. I won a talent scholarship in the non-finalist competitions, and that money would take me a long, long way.

Learning to Starve

Food has never been that big a deal to me—the simpler, the better. I'm no gourmand like my husband, who loves long, exquisitely prepared meals. Me, I'd rather spend my time shopping for clothes and things. Plus, I've always been more of a down-home diner kind of gal than the fancy restaurant type. Basically, I have five favorite foods, and two of them are potatoes. My big thing in Orlando was to go to Steak'n Shake. I had to sneak over there during the pageant years because I wasn't supposed to be having that stuff.

After the Miss America pageant, I went home to fulfill my duties as Miss Florida. I made money for each public appearance ($50 to $150 a pop), so I was busy zipping all over the state of Florida in my pageant Toyota like a little cash register. One day I'd be doing telethons and the next I'd be kissing Shamu the whale—it didn't matter. All I wanted was to be out in front of the people. I did commercials on local television with Bill Baer, "Mr. Color TV," selling TV sets in skits such as "Goldilocks and the Three Baers." I ended up with almost ten thousand dollars, counting my talent scholarship from the Miss America pageant, and a TV from Bill Baer.

At the end of the year I had to do what has always been the toughest part of my reigns: give up my crown. When it came time to give up a crown, I never wanted to let go. Once I had, I was always tempted to snatch it back and run off the stage. Plus, it kills me how they always want to shove the old queens in back, out of the picture, the second they've picked a new queen. But in the back of my mind I knew this would be my swan song as a beauty queen, and I went down without a fight.

I felt I should have a plan for the rest of my life, so not having a clear plan, or *any* plan for that matter, made me anxious, and I started to gain weight. I got up to 155 pounds. It got to the point where I was afraid to go out; I was afraid of what "the public" would see. I holed up in my room because I was ashamed, because people gave me such grief about it. I was safe, being heavy. I didn't have to deal with the sexual stuff. I receded into a big, comfortable shell.

Good-bye, Steak 'n Shake—Hello, London

It's traditional for beauty queens to use their pageant money toward educational expenses. This I did—but instead of choosing a college, I decided on acting lessons. One choice was going to New York to study, but even I recognized that I wasn't ready for that. Up until then I had been living a sheltered, idyllic life—isolated, surrounded by chaperones, treated like a princess.

I went out on a limb and applied to the London Academy of Music and Dramatic Arts. I thought some sort of classical training would beef up my credentials. I was accepted and ended up spending almost two years studying acting in London. Although London was way across on the other side of the world—about as far away from Orlando, Florida, as you can get—it was a much gentler place for a young girl to live alone than someplace like New York City. In London, I was allowed to mature and develop my own identity in a leisurely fashion. I did a lot of growing up there.

❝ *We sent over this little innocent pageant girl, my husband and I. He said, 'I'm terrified of leaving her here.' So was I. But she was so determined.* ❞ —Jean Burke

A Dramatic Entrance . . .

London is where I first discovered those troublesome diet pills, black beauties, to be specific. The pills made my heart race, so in order to keep from fainting I would have to stop at every landing on the steps to school. To make things worse, I'd have nothing to eat all day. Then I would go back to my room and open up one can of macaroni and cheese with some diet crackers. It was a good day if I consumed 800 calories. But it sure seemed worth it: I got down to 112 pounds and a size 6. I was thrilled—even my legs were skinny! I remember being invited to a fancy dinner party and making what I thought was a dramatic entrance at the top of some very elegant stairs. I hadn't had any real food in a while, and the next thing I remember, I'm at the bottom of the stairs, passed out, having fallen from the top to the bottom. Waking up, I noticed that I was *not* in a position one wants to be found in when passing out—my butt was up in the air, you know. I came to long enough to know this was not how I'd want to be found. I managed to roll myself over and position my arms and legs before passing out again. I was then found lying in a *very* dramatic fashion on the floor—passed out, underfed, but looking good in a size-6 faint.

. . . And Exit: The Woman in Black

I was only nineteen when I went to London and was always the youngest in the class—back in school and once again very much alone in trying to sort a lot of things out. To the faculty I was pretty and I was sexy—therefore, I must be stupid. That's how they viewed me. They'd give all the juicy dramatic parts to other women. It would frustrate me, but it was also educational. I had no idea then how it was preparing me for Hollywood. In London I was often surrounded by smugly

self-confident people, and with my pink pageant makeup cases and color-coordinated outfits I was an easy target. I was so naive I called them "suede-o-intellectuals."

But I was also ready to let go of the beauty queen image. I recognized that people often equate that image with being plastic and empty-headed—and treat you accordingly.

I kept trying to prove myself as an actress in school, fighting to do emotionally wrenching roles like Lady Macbeth and Blanche du Bois. The English would say "Isn't she wonderful" and "Such marvelous instincts," but then they would try to change my acting style into something more English, more technical—and not how I work at all. I wondered, Why do you praise my work and then try to change me?

One thing that did evolve rapidly was my look. I became what you'd call *flamboyant*. I reinvented myself. I had flown into town in my Miss Florida wardrobe with the little hairpiece and pageant do and matching hat, shoes, and bag—very put together. By the time I left I was wearing only black—black hat, black veil, black cape, black gloves, boots, dress, you name it. I let my hair grow long and go wild.

In some sense, I realize now, I dressed this way as a natural defense mechanism. I was tired of people following me on the street. I was still traumatized by fear and didn't understand or accept the power and responsibility of beauty. When you have it, you usually don't know you have it. It's confusing. Why were people bothering me? I didn't know at the time how to turn that thinking around, to use the power. I mean, sex was the scariest thing I could think of—no way was I ready for it emotionally—and yet here was this fully developed body projecting pure, unadulterated sexuality. I didn't know how to handle it. The reactions I got disturbed and confounded me.

I was unusually trusting and naive, which I continue to be to this day. I was very firm about the direction of my career and how to develop my talents, however; I was much older in my ambitions. Otherwise, I was a child. In spite of my mother's warnings about predators and "Do you really want to be in this business?" I was off in my fantasy land, not realizing the effect I was having on people. I didn't know why these nice old gentlemen who presented themselves as father figures would suddenly be pressing themselves against me.

I look back on that time, from the age of fourteen to twenty, a time of youth, a time of beauty, a time of hope and unexplored opportunities, and upon reflection I think that like me, most young women are unable to handle that power or deal with suddenly being fair game in the sexual hunt.

Women my age were handed a double whammy in the 1970s, as sexual roles were being shuffled and rearranged. Here I was, barely twenty years old, emotionally naive and all dewy-eyed, living far from home for the first time in my life. And society was sending this message of "anything goes." And by sending this message, it put pressure on young women at a time when most didn't have a clue what they wanted and didn't realize they had the power to choose.

By the time I had it figured out, I was in my thirties, and boy, had my body changed. I didn't look the same kind of pretty; I had a different look. I coveted what I used to be. I would look back on those pictures when I was younger, when everyone was telling me how fat I was, and realize I was a damn goddess—but I also liked the emotional growth that had happened to me along the way. So although I had lost the effortless physical power I had enjoyed in my youth, I discovered I had developed emotional and intellectual power. It was all so much richer.

Today when I look at young girls, girls in their twenties, in the full bloom of youth, I can truly admire their lush skin and easy beauty—and at the same time I think, No way would I trade places.

❝ *When Delta came back home, and we went to pick her up at the airport, we were expecting our little Delta. Off the ramp walks this woman, with black cape flowing and a black hat with*

*the brim down, a black walking stick with silver top, and vivid
red lipstick. And people are looking, saying, 'Who's that, who's
that?' She drew a lot of attention. She went to London basically
a girl and came back a woman.* —Jennifer Burke, Delta's sister

Hollywood, the Camera, and Food

After London, I decided it was time to go to Los Angeles. I
remember some friends coming by to see me in Orlando to
say good-bye. These weren't *real* friends; these were the ones
who had made fun of me when I put on the weight. So I
would meet them at the door half dressed—my skirt on, and
my bra, but not my shirt, so they could really see how thin I'd
gotten. Thinner even than when I was in pageants, and it just
made them sick with envy. By this time my mother was beg-
ging me to eat. That was kind of thrilling: It was the first time
in my life that anyone had begged me to eat. And I said, no,
I'm not going to eat, because choosing not to eat was in my
power. I felt *in control.*

If you saw pictures of me then, you would hardly know it
was me. I weighed only 110 or 112 pounds. I was still starving
myself and taking black beauties, which made me dizzy and my
heart race. My mother says she was always finding me passed
out over some potted plant.

I drove out to Los Angeles with my grandmother Nana in
an old yellow Pontiac Firebird, toting a U-Haul. Nana had a
gun under the seat, because she had heard that bandits could
ambush you in the desert. I was scared to death the whole way
because the safety on the gun was broken. No sooner had we
gotten to Los Angeles than we were welcomed by an earth-
quake.

Before going, I had written SAG (Screen Actors Guild) for a
list of agents. Armed with this list, I would stay up till the middle
of the night, typing away at résumés, sending out 8-by-10
glossies. I had written some five hundred people in Los Angeles

before leaving Orlando. I even got a service number in L.A., with a perky message saying, "I'll be in town on May second. You all can reach me at this number." I was expecting a big response. What did I know?

But those are the special years when you don't know you can fail. I thought big—I *knew* I would be famous. So though I was emotionally young and naive, my drive was fully formed. I had a strong sense of direction and of who I wanted to be and what I wanted to do.

So I really wasn't surprised when I got to L.A. and, lo and behold, there *were* messages for me and people setting up auditions and appointments. I was a very busy new girl in town who didn't know better. Still being in my London theatrical mode, I would show up for auditions wearing black gypsy or pirate outfits. I even wore riding habits to auditions—I *loved* riding habits. I walked around in black seamed stockings and high-heeled shoes. They didn't know what to make of me in Los Angeles, but they really liked me.

My real first break resulted from an act of sheer kindness. Hollywood's legendary casting director Eddie Foy III had been a judge at the 1974 Miss America pageant, and after the pageant he had said, "Look me up if you ever go to Hollywood." Is that a classic line or what? I of course took him at face value, and once I got to Hollywood, I just rang Mr. Eddie Foy III up. Amazingly, he said come on in. While I was sitting in his office, he rang up two or three agents who liked new faces and recommended me on the spot. Even more amazingly, one of those people soon thereafter took me on as a client. All in all, a classy leap of faith from Mr. Foy—for which I am forever indebted.

I was sent out on casting calls. Being a pretty quick study, I recognized which "auditions" were for real acting jobs and which were for something else altogether. The latter were the kind where the waiting room was filled with models and showgirl types. Sitting in the room with all these beautiful women made me feel like I was back in that first-grade class-room. I didn't feel I could compete with them on a physical level, and the parts were nothing, so I wouldn't be able to show off any acting ability. Even then, I was self-aware enough to know that mine was a combination of looking good enough and being able to act well enough. To make matters even more disturbing, many of these auditions required the girls to take their clothes off. I would see the girls wrecked and nervous, wrestling with the situation in their heads: Should I do it or not? There was a certain desperation in their eyes, as if they felt they had little choice in the matter. So some would just give in to it. And I was very uncomfortable being viewed on just a physical level, and I didn't like the way these places made me feel. So I asked my agent to stop sending me to those kinds of auditions.

Years later, when an infamous tell-all book written by Hollywood call girls and prostitutes came out, I thumbed through the book, thinking, That could have been me. One thing that saved me: Even way back then I had a real mission, and I believed enough in my abilities to keep me going. Had I not had a single-minded sense of direction, theirs could easily have been my fate. More important was a solid family founda-tion instilled from the day I was born; if you don't have a sup-portive upbringing, it's easy to lose yourself in Hollywood.

There I was, at twenty-one, showing up at film and TV auditions in sexy black stockings and short skirts and going home to my grandmother at night. I didn't really date. I didn't get out and meet a lot of men. I was still hiding from real life, but I didn't realize it at the time, for I was too busy driving my career forward. My grandmother was the safe harbor I needed and returned to each evening.

And what, might you ask, did we do with our time together? We spent a lot of time trying out new recipes—I remember making some kind of godawful tomato aspic—and rearranging furniture and the posters of Vivien Leigh and

Marilyn Monroe I hung on the walls. We'd visit the farmers' market and comb the streets, finding perfectly good furniture that people had left on the side of the road. I still have a table in my upstairs parlor that Nana and I hauled home. Once I got work, however, we moved up the social ladder a bit. My grandmother never ceased to thrill at being waved through the gates of Paramount Studios. After all our dreams.

Chewing the Scenery

I had amazing fortune my first year in Hollywood, 1978. The first month I got a one-line bit part in a TV movie called *Zuma Beach,* but my scene ended up on the cutting room floor. One month later I won a supporting role in a movie called *Cry for Help.* The third month, following a big studio search for an unknown Scarlett O'Hara/Vivien Leigh type (just like the Scarlett search years ago in the making of *Gone With the Wind*), I won the lead in the movie-pilot episode for a series, *Charleston.* This, in Hollywood lingo, was my big break.

There I was, at twenty-two, selected from thousands of girls to carry a big-budget television series with high-profile publicity. I remember being determined to stay thin, so for me, feeling cold, clammy, and dizzy from not eating was the norm. I'd even pass out occasionally at fittings. My happiest moment was fitting into a belt that had been worn by Audrey Hepburn. I was so proud!

I hit the set raring to go, but as the production rolled along it became apparent to me and everyone else on the set that I hadn't yet learned how to act in front of the camera. I was stage acting, which for television is overacting. Well, I was overacting *all over the place.* The directors, bless them, just closed their eyes and turned me loose, letting me chew up the scenery doing bad Vivien Leigh imitations.

After the filming was completed, I sneaked into a preview, wearing a wig and sunglasses. A test audience was brought in to

3
5

weigh in on the production and was asked to push buttons whenever actors came on to show who they liked and didn't like. I spent the night turning my button *way* up every time I came on. But this guy next to me for some reason hated my guts. Every time I'd come on the screen he'd press that negative button. And I'm thinking, I should just rip off my wig and look him in the eye and say, "Do you have any idea how miserable you are making me?" But I didn't. I thought, well, they gave Ann-Margret

I won the coveted role as the "unknown" in Charleston.

Photofest (Charleston, miniseries)

a hard time too, and I'll just rise above it like she did. But it was *very* hard to be exposed to all that public criticism.

When *Charleston* aired, there were few surprises. The series was a stinker, and I was panned big time. I'd go to the grocery store or an audition and hear, "Boy, did I see a turkey last night, called *Charleston.*" In my business, you learn your lessons in a very public way.

❝ *She could easily become a star, because she has several of the necessary ingredients. To name two: she is one of the most beautiful women to come to town in a long time. And second, she is a little offbeat in some ways.* **❞**

—Dick Kleiner, Newspaper Enterprise Association

Queen of the Guest Stars

There weren't many 1980s TV shows I didn't make an appearance on. I even made return engagements: I was on *The Love Boat* three times. Nine times out of ten, my character was an oversexed vamp. I changed in and out of an awful lot of nightgowns. Here are a few backstage snapshots.

The Seekers. This miniseries featured some of my first seduction scenes. Mother and Dad, watching at home, were somewhat nonplussed. Dad turned to Mom, with a look of astonishment on his face. "My God, Jean—Delta's sexy!" Because none of us had a clue.

The Chisholms. In 1980, I won a lead in the CBS western television series *The Chisholms,* in which I played Bonnie Sue Chisholm, the stoic daughter of a pioneer family crossing the frontier in a covered wagon. My character was always pregnant, and I was always gazing lovingly at a new baby—which was really a doll—and then looking at my husband and then back to the doll. I must have gazed at that doll for months. No wonder I sometimes felt like dropping it under the wagon wheels.

Remington Steele. The thing that stands out from my guest appearance on *Remington Steele,* besides my really bad perm, is how incredibly, wonderfully nice Pierce Brosnan was. I thought, How can such a handsome guy be that easygoing and down to earth? And with all his success, he has stayed that nice guy. In my episode, an amnesiac wanted for murder finds he has five lives with five different wives. I, of course, played the oversexed, easily seduced, money-hungry wife.

The Love Boat. I did this show three times, and in one of them I have a bed scene with Doc, which was a comedy in itself. When you did *The Love Boat* you were coated with tan body makeup; it was called the "Love Boat Glow." I have nothing but happy memories of doing *The Love Boat,* though. It was a fun, whimsical show and gave me a chance to work on comedy timing.

Mike Hammer. I was so excited to be working with the talented Stacy Keach that I had an attack of nerves. But before I could get to work, there were more pressing matters to deal with. Jay Bernstein, the producer, liked to make sure that all the women hired to appear on the show had that "Mike Hammer Look"—which meant that no matter how big your bosoms were, you would be padded to make them bigger. So by the time I was ready for my first scene, I was not only padded in the front but stuffed on the sides too. I was bumping into *everything.* That only added to my nervousness, and when I'm *really* nervous, my voice gets Marilyn Monroe high and squeaky. That voice betrays me every time. So out I walk, padded out to here, trussed up like a Christmas turkey, and talking like I just inhaled a tankful of helium.

Luckily, Keach was a very nice guy, and he immediately made me feel relaxed. He was great fun and we worked well together.

The Fall Guy. In this 1982 episode, I played a carnival performer trying to save an orangutan accused of murder from being destroyed. You know how murderous those orangutans can be. Off the set, everyone hated that orangutan. He had a bad habit of peeing on people's shoes.

Fantasy Island. In the episode I starred in, I wore tight outfits and did my usual snippy talk and fast walk, and because I was the villain I got to smoke a lot of cigarettes. Ricardo Montalban was a real gentleman, and I vaguely recall his having Spanish music playing constantly on the set.

Nero Wolfe. William Conrad was a fine actor, but when I worked with him he read his lines from cue cards and never looked at the other actors. Just the way he worked, I guess, but a bit disconcerting.

A Bunny's Tale. In this TV movie I played a Playboy bunny who was proud of her body. She was really out there, all saucy and sassy. Kirstie Alley starred in it, and she had the bright idea that we should all dress up as men at the wrap party. She felt we had suffered enough in those bunny outfits, having been ogled incessantly by the crew and made to hold our bladders all day—those outfits made going to the bathroom a big production. The whole crew got into it; the wardrobe people tailored men's outfits to fit us, and the makeup and hair people really did a number on us to make us look authentically male. Aside from having to keep my hot pink fingernails in my trousers the whole night, I looked pretty good.

Temporary Insanity. One of my favorite roles ever, in a film that was never shown. I played a dominatrix named Big

Woman, and I got to do a lot of spoofy sexy shtick. Richard Lewis costarred, and I was bent on seducing him in nearly every scene. But it was hard to keep a straight face doing my seduction stuff because he kept making up hilarious new dialogue in midstream. At that time, I had a tendency to carry a role with me long after it was over. By the time we finished filming I had got so used to tight leather skirts and stiletto heels that I just didn't feel like myself without them.

Recognize me? I'm dressed in drag for the wrap party for A Bunny's Tale, a TV movie about Playboy bunnies. Collection of Delta Burke

Guess the Show. It was common knowledge in Hollywood that the big star of a TV series I was slated to appear on had the habit of hitting on all the actresses who came on the set. Of course, I knew nothing of this at the time; I was too busy picking up used furniture off the highway with my grandmother! I found out soon enough: In my first week on the set, Big Star informs me very matter-of-factly about the affair we are going to have; he even has an apartment all set up. So while I'm

Playing a leather-clad, over-the-top dominatrix in Temporary Insanity *was liberating and fun.* Collection of Delta Burke

trying to avoid dealing with this, I'm having to act with this guy and not incur his wrath. I mean, I was a *nobody*. So one day on the set he says to me that the time has come: I am, as he put it, "this week's meat."

What could I possibly say that would put the brakes on the galloping libido of a semirational man? "I can't deal with this right now," I lied. "I was recently raped."

I could hear Big Star swallow a guffaw. "I'll help you get over it," he said leeringly.

Years later, when I was nominated for my first Emmy, I ran into Big Aging Star at the awards show. He barely acknowledged me. "Whadda ya know?" I silently cheered. "This week's meat just made the big time."

Over the years, I learned comedic timing and faces from watching Carol Burnett. So when I finally did her show, I looked like a monkey mimicking the master: We had identical comic reactions—well, not exactly identical but the best I could manage. Photofest (Carol Burnett)

One of my first jobs was an extra in Disney's *The Treasure of Matecumbe*, filmed in Florida. Here I am with Peter Ustinov.

Photofest (The Treasure of Matecumbe)

I learned to twirl a gun in *Gun Shy*. Not easy with long nails!

Photofest (Gun Shy)

Filthy Rich: Suzanne in the Beginning

The first time I met the writer/producer Linda Bloodworth-Thomason and the actress Dixie Carter was when I shot the pilot for *Filthy Rich*. Linda was a well-respected comedy writer who was writing and directing the pilot, and I was twenty-four years old. I read the script, thought it was hysterically funny, and agreed to do it. It was about an ex–beauty queen who marries an old man for his money, and then during sex he dies. He is cryogenically frozen, and his whole family is forced to live under one roof—and none of that motley crew approves of me, the gold-digging young wife, younger even than my stepson and daughter-in-law, played by Dixie. That character was an early, raw version of *Designing Women*'s Suzanne Sugarbaker.

Before I got the part people said, "Oh, Delta Burke, she doesn't do comedy." So at the audition I decided to play up my pageant background. I wore a little Dolly Parton–style dotted swiss dress to the audition that was lowcut and had little white bows that tied at the bust and puffy sleeves right up to the elbow. I had my hair in a Vivien Leigh do, *Gone With the Wind* style, with the hair held up on the sides by combs and bows.

Linda loved the look; it made her feel I was her kind of gal. So with a little help from that puffy-sleeved getup, I got the part.

The seeds of my personal and professional growth were planted then. At the time, my personal identity was still tied into being Miss Florida. I knew how to smile and say all the right things. But I still hadn't discovered how to be myself. With *Filthy Rich*, I found a new persona to get lost in. I became more adept at using my voice, more proficient at comedic timing, and more natural with my rhythm. The show was an over-the-top spoof of the soaps, and I was free to grow and develop my innate comedic talents. I was a natural clown, and I loved making an audience laugh.

It was a tremendous learning experience as well. I spent a lot of time watching Dixie and costar Ann Wedgworth run their paces. From them I truly began to learn comedy. I would also like to give credit to all my costars on *Designing Women*—Dixie Carter, Annie Potts, Jean Smart, Mesach Taylor, and the "little fruitcake," Alice Ghostley. The finest cast ever assembled. I learned so much about comedy (rhythm, timing, inflection, pacing, and so on) from each of them. When you turned us loose, it was a breeding ground for comedy. To learn to do good ensemble comedic work is one of the biggest highs of my life.

❝*In the beginning Delta didn't really know what she was doing, but she was so instinctively good, it almost didn't matter. All the instruments were in place. And her beauty! I remember being in the control room with the then president of Columbia Pictures watching scenes from Filthy Rich. Delta came on in an evening gown, and that executive said, 'That is the most beautiful human being I have ever seen.' But even at her most beautiful, it seemed that women liked her even better than men did, which is unusual for gorgeous women. She is so sweet and has such a good heart that women want to be her buddy; they feel they can open up to her. And she was never sure of her beauty. Compliments meant a lot to her because she was never quite confident enough. You'd say she looked nice, and she'd be truly flattered. 'Really?' she'd say. And you'd think: Did you take a look in the mirror this morning?*❞ —Linda Bloodworth-Thomason

At that point, I wasn't big but I wasn't exactly a size 6 either. I had put some weight back on, and I started to hear about it. My body normally wanted to stay at an 8 or a 10, which would have been fine if I left it alone, but I kept trying to make it a 6. That's when I discovered crystal meth, a powerful amphetamine that cut my hunger but made my heart race. I would literally pass out when I stood up. It had the unfortunate side effect of making me paranoid, so I stopped taking it after a few months. So, when I was working in front of the camera I went back to starving myself, sometimes going without food for five days. It would get to the point where if I ate just a salad after skipping dinner for a couple of days, I couldn't fit into my clothes to shoot the episodes.

Even then, I was losing parts because of my "weight problem" and becoming the subject of catty remarks. I even overheard another actress on *The Chisholms* set say, "Jeez, if I keep eating like this I'm gonna look as fat as Delta." When I went to lunch on the set, I would get some type of snide comment regardless of what I did. If I ate anything, I'd get "You shouldn't be eating." If I didn't eat, I'd hear, "Oh she's starving again; how sad."

In this business, you're made to feel that being less than perfect is disastrous, and there is always someone playing with your head about it. Young girls in particular are vulnerable. Whether it is people offering advice or just trying to be funny, it becomes really mean and hurtful.

The thing is, when I look back at television footage from that time, I was a goddess. And I didn't even know it. How could I let them convince me that I wasn't thin enough and I wasn't beautiful enough? Why did I believe them?

A Swinger in Malibu

When I wasn't working, I was sleeping. Or recovering from work. Or doing the constant beauty maintenance. Again, I did not date. Who had the time?

But time was only part of it. I was not wise to the ways of the world at all. I might play sexy parts, but in reality I was not what I was cast. Some people were, shall we say, a mite confused by that. I know I was. And I wasn't cynical enough to go the casting couch route or use people to forward my career.

I was invited to several parties in Malibu, where the famous hung out. The houses were dreamy, hanging right there over the Pacific Ocean, and lots of beautiful women were recruited to decorate the surroundings. That was the first time I saw drugs laid about like so much salsa and dip. One famous actor with a reputation as a lady killer was helping himself to the goodies and asking for my telephone number at the same time. Being naive, I gave it to him. Later I told some more seasoned actresses about it, and they listed about a hundred reasons why I should not go out with a guy like that. I needed all one hundred of them to bolster my confidence to say no. So I was spared from going down *that* road.

Mark Rydell, the director of *On Golden Pond,* took it upon himself to be very protective of me at those parties. It just might have had something to do with how out of place I seemed at one Malibu home, holding tight onto a script so everyone would know that I was a serious actress. Mark knew I looked more like fresh meat than anything else, and he kept the wolves away from me, God bless him!

I could easily have been taken advantage of because I was always reacting to other people's expectations of me rather than acting on what I felt. Once again, I felt out of control and handled it the only way I knew how: to go home to Nana and shut down. This was a world where people were not only playing but playing *for keeps*. It was a game I didn't feel comfortable playing, so I just stopped going to those parties after a while.

❝ *Delta has a special quality of endearment. Good people want to take care of her, not take advantage of her. It's rare for someone to have been in the business as long and as successfully as Delta has and yet remain unspoiled.* ❞ —Martin Hurwitz, Beverly Hills agent

I was lucky in that I've always had protective people around me. And as I've matured and felt more comfortable with myself, I've been able to choose those people rather than rely on luck. At the time, though, I was as green as they come in the ways of the world, let alone the jungle of Hollywood. I remember a very well-known producer literally jumping me in the hallway of a studio one day and being completely shocked at his audacity. In retrospect, the signs were there all along. But I was so naive and unable to express my feelings that you had to either physically pounce on me in a hallway or put it on a billboard for me to get it.

I remember one movie executive in particular who would come on to me and call me Kathleen, my *Filthy Rich* character's name. Really, I thought, you'd think that people who make their living making movies could tell the difference between myth and reality. But then why should I have thought that? I wasn't so hot at it myself.

Filthy Rich was canceled. Even after being a number-one smash as a summer fill-in, when it returned to the fall schedule, the viewers left. I then went on to play the lead in an HBO series, *First and Ten*. I played the female owner of a football team, which was certainly a departure for me—for once I was not the town floozy.

I got the role of a woman football-team owner in the HBO series First and Ten. Photofest (First and Ten)

If anything, that part got me out of nightgowns. I was going to research the part—you know, learn a little football lingo—so when guys off the set would hear what I was working on, I could share football stats with aplomb. But even after doing twelve episodes of *First and Ten,* I didn't have the slightest idea what they were talking about. To make matters even more complicated, *Designing Women* came along about that time, and at one point I was doing them both at the same time. I'd rush from playing one character rattling on about lateral passes to another swooning over pedicures.

A word about sets: Your social life revolves around whatever show, whatever sitcom, whatever movie you're making at the time. Everyone becomes family very quickly. Most of my relationships in Los Angeles came through work—anyone I dated, any one of my close circle of friends. So when I would go to work on other shows and wouldn't hear from those friends, it hurt. I had to come to grips with the fact that it wasn't personal, it wasn't that they didn't like me anymore. I'd go off and do another show and make a new family, and the unending process continually repeated itself.

That's not to say that I didn't make lasting friends in Los Angeles. I miss in particular Jean Smart, Mesach Taylor, and many of the prop and wardrobe people I worked with on *Designing Women.* When you have enough work that you keep running into these same people again and again, it's nice— you're returning to the family fold. You begin to feel like you're one of the town's real troopers.

Linda and Designing Women

When Linda Bloodworth-Thomason created the situation comedy *Designing Women,* she was smart enough to bring together the characters that Dixie and I had played on *Filthy Rich* and the same characters that Annie Potts and Jean Smart had played for Linda on a short-lived 1985 series called *Lime Street* and put them all in an interior design firm set in Atlanta.

I of course played Suzanne Sugarbaker, the sassy, self-absorbed ex–beauty queen who is selfish but honest to a fault. Dixie played my wise older sister, Julia Sugarbaker.

The show's premise was deceptively simple ("Get four women together and listen to them talk," Linda once said). But Linda had a definite agenda on her mind, a couple of underlying themes she wanted to drive home. One was to dispense with the Southern stereotypes that the entertainment industry had fed the public for years—what she called "hick-bashing." Someone once said that Linda's aim was to put forth the idea of the Southern woman who is not sitting on a front porch in her slip scratching herself. And, having

Designing Women in Southern belle outfits. Photofest (Designing Women)

worked as a writer on the highly successful sitcom *M.A.S.H.*, Linda wanted to show that women enjoy the same kind of bantering and camaraderie that men do. It helps when the women are as smart and strong and funny as our characters were drawn.

Although Annie Potts used to say that our characters were all separate facets of Linda's personality, it was Julia Sugarbaker who was Linda's mouthpiece. Julia was able to tell off anyone who deserved to be told off—and do it with Southern charm. Linda then placed into the mix Mesach Taylor, the very funny actor who played Anthony Bouvier, the design firm's black delivery-man. Over time, Anthony and Suzanne developed a kinship that made them one of TV's oddest but most endearing couples.

The show was very much a collaboration, and we each brought pieces of our own personality to our characters. I remember Jean being frustrated during the first season. She felt that her character was not clearly defined—one week she'd be ditsy; the next week she'd be smart, the same as with my character. "Look," I told Jean, "it's a comedy. Whatever Linda gives you, *just make it funny*." Linda would see something we'd do in real life and latch on to it—I'd see her constantly scribbling furiously in longhand on that yellow pad—and it became part of the character. And that's how our characters grew. Over the course of the years, Jean and I personally evolved the most, and you can see that growth reflected in our characters.

Not only was Linda tuned in to my innermost thoughts and feelings, but she became my creative mother. I think we fueled each other's creativity. She often said she could write the best and easiest for my character—she heard Suzanne in her head all the time.

❝ *Suzanne was selfish and self-absorbed and she was always saying politically incorrect things—but Delta had such a likable, innocent quality that she got away with it. She didn't come across as mean-spirited.* ❞ —Linda Bloodworth-Thomason

At the same time, Nana became too sick to live with me—she was suffering from progressive kidney disease—and she went home to live with my mother. So for the next few years I looked to Dixie Carter and Linda as mother, mentor, sister—you name it. I don't think they knew what to do with me. I was the baby—the youngest actress on the set—and somewhat needy. I was used to having a lot of family around, and because of that, I

I love Mesach, and I must say he makes a formidable-looking woman.

Photofest (Delta and Mesach).

remained very open and trusting. So I relied on my friends on the set. Dixie would have me over for weekends and cook soup for me and call me Delta Dawn. Annie brought me chicken soup when I was sick. I remember there being a lot of soup.

Right from the beginning of *Designing Women,* I decided to make the most, careerwise, of the opportunity while I could. Of the shows I had previously starred in, none had lasted more than a year. Just when I would be getting settled in and reaching for the phone to hire a press agent—usually about the thirteenth episode—somebody would go and cancel the thing. So when this one came along, I thought, hell, I'm going to get a publicist and get my name out there right from the start and not wait for someone to cancel the show. I figured this was my big break, and so, whether the show was successful or not, by God, I was going to get name recognition! That's why I ended up on *Hollywood Squares* and morning shows and ribbon cuttings all over the country. I was out there hustling. And by the year's end, wouldn't you know it, the public knew who I was.

❝*The networks did not want Delta for the part at first. That was one of the conditions in doing the pilot: No Delta. But once we started shooting we realized pretty quickly that the actress we got in her place was not working out. So twenty-four hours before we were to shoot the pilot in front of a live audience, I went to the network people in desperation. If one person doesn't work, I said, then the whole thing doesn't work—the characters are so intertwined.*

They let me make the call. So I let the other actress go and called Delta, who was on the other side of the country, and said, 'You have to come out and read for this right now.'

***Hours later, she came barreling into the studio, and I took her aside and we were both chattering away: 'We can do this! It's you—it's your part!' And she went out and did it.*❞**

—Linda Bloodworth-Thomason

5
3

The critics and the audience loved the show. Even so, the network, as networks will do, moved it all over the schedule and was on the verge of canceling it in the spring of 1987. When news leaked of the show's impending doom, it was a massive letter-writing campaign and hard work that saved it from the wrecking ball. We got another shot, and from then on, *Designing Women* built a solid audience, shot up in the ratings, and became a top-ten hit.

❝*A hip, sharp contemporary comedy about modern, urban Southern women.*❞ —Robert P. Laurence, *San Diego Union Tribune*

❝**Designing Women** *proved that wit exists outside New York, Los Angeles, Boston, and Washington.*❞
—Mike Boone, *Montreal Gazette*

❝*Done in a very sharp, very clever way. It's just a very savvy show*.❞ —Larry Gelbart, former producer of *M.A.S.H.*

❝*A shrewd sitcom.*❞ —John J. O'Connor, *New York Times*

We were all swept along by its success. The show was featured in every national publication in the country, from *People* to *USA Today*. "Delta Dawns as Belle of the Sitcom," read a *Chicago Tribune* headline in March 1987. I remember doing a little war dance at a newsstand in Cleveland when I first saw myself on the cover of *TV Guide*. "You Think Her Character Is Outlandish? Meet the Real Delta Burke!" the headline trumpeted.

❝*When Delta Burke sweeps into a restaurant, heads turn and talk stops. . . . [She] wears a shocking pink and white low-cut dress that fits so closely you think she may have been shrink-wrapped. Her shoes are matching pink and white, her bag pink, her hair puffed like cotton candy. . . . As she approaches the table, she extracts a lace fan from her purse, peers coyly over it and says in tones of pure magnolia, 'Pleased to meet y'all.'* 99

—Edwin Kiester, Jr., *TV Guide*

I'm surprised the reporter stayed for lunch. "I have a streak of white trash," I said, fanning myself. "I think it's in my blood. When I go out I want to look all elegant and like a lady, but by the time I reach the door I look like a lady of the evening." I even had the naïveté to drop a half-eaten sandwich into my purse as I left the restaurant—which the interviewer duly noted.

I'll admit: I was flamboyant, a ham, honest to a fault, with a flair for the dramatic. But even then I played with that persona; it was a spoof, and I was happy to be entertaining folks by juggling to be the person everyone wanted me to be. This was the big time, damn it, what I had been working for my whole life. I turned thirty years old that year.

66 *No character evolved as much as Suzanne did during the first five years—and no actress evolved as quickly as Delta did. You can see, in the pilot for* **Designing Women,** *that she wasn't quite sure of herself. But you could watch her confidence growing by leaps and bounds every week. We all just sat around with our mouths open and watched this star emerge. Pretty soon, she would just walk into a room during a taping and people would start clapping.* 99 —Linda Bloodworth-Thomason

That Thing About Weight

When I think back to the beginning of *Designing Women,* my life was like a carousel that was going faster and faster. The show made me famous—I thought I had what I wanted. What's that old saying? Be careful what you wish for—you just might get it.

Every now and then, "the weight" became an issue. Regardless of what size I was, I was convinced I looked plain awful. Even when I was a size 6, I'd hear complaints that my hips were too curvy or my legs too big. And I bought into the whole thing. I'd get up to 123 or 133 pounds and think, I'm such a cow. And I look back now and say, "My God, I was a beautiful, curvy woman, and I was never even aware of it."

For a long time, I tried to be what they wanted me to be. Let's see, how many "diet" programs did I go through? There was something called the Lindora program, where you were injected with something like pregnant women's urine and fed powdered drinks. There was the Pritikin Center program, where I'd go to lose a lot of weight quickly. They'd have activities like Dress-Up Day, and I'd bring my crowns, boas, and wigs and dress everyone up while we worked out on our treadmills. Well, we had to have some kind of entertainment—I mean, they weren't feeding us! There were the diet shakes, the stimulants—you name it, I tried it. Unfortunately, I found that starvation was the one thing that successfully whittled me down to a size 6.

The "weight problem" was something I couldn't ignore even if I wanted to. The issue was forced on me. When I was doing the *Designing Women* pilot, the image that sticks in my mind is me out there in the middle of the stage, with everybody looking at me, moving around me, and judging how I looked in outfits. "How," they asked, holding up their hands, "can we cover up those big old thighs?" Talking about me like I was some piece of meat who couldn't hear what they were saying.

But I never felt that "the weight" could affect my livelihood until the wedding of Jean Smart and Richard Gilliland, the actor who played Annie Potts's boyfriend on the show. It was the end of the first season, and we were all invited, and I sat with a big group of people from *Designing Women*. Suddenly a crew member whispered to me that the word on the set was that I had better lose some weight or I was going to get fired. And that the word was coming down from the "network people."

I was stunned. That was the first I'd heard about any ulti-
matums from the networks. Of course, I believed the rumor to
be true and decided to do what I have always done: diet, starve,
faint, whatever it takes. I'll work, do interviews, do readings,
make appearances, all without eating. I had the dreaded sense
of *here we go again.*

At the same time, I remember going on a personal appearance tour and hearing some comments that struck me as odd.
Large-size women were coming up to me and saying, "Your
success means a lot to us" and "We finally have someone we

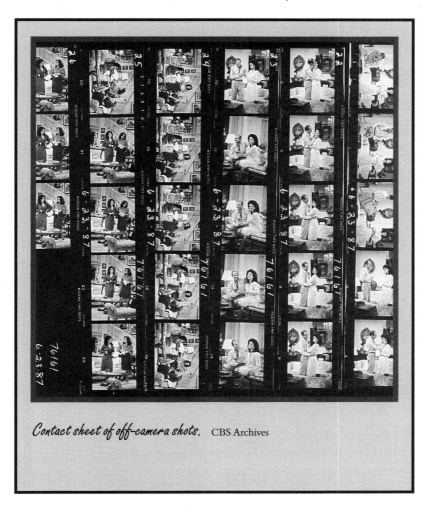

Contact sheet of off-camera shots. CBS Archives

can relate to." That kind of threw me: I didn't think of myself that way—at least, not yet.

Mac

One thing that hadn't changed was my status as a single woman. My life in Hollywood had been a replay of high school days: work, career, maintenance. I rarely dated; I didn't have time, and I was more than a little intimidated by the whole thing. The dating scene in Hollywood was not exactly something you could just "ease into." In fact, on one occasion I found myself in a situation that could be called date rape. I had jumped into a tank full of piranhas. Because of my past, I was doubly uncomfortable, and yet I kept looking to other people to clue me in on what was expected of me. And I was shocked to discover that the message of what was expected of me often bordered on the obscene.

Oh, I talked a tough game. Here I am in 1986 justifying my social life to the *Dallas Morning News:*

If I can't have what I want, I would just as soon not have anything. I'm a loner anyway. I like being alone, and unless I can share my life the way I want to share it, then it's wasted time to me. So I don't have to have that to feel complete. And I really resent people thinking that you're not complete unless you have the matching bookends. . . . The easiest thing to do is get married.

Not six months later, I was attending a press luncheon at the Beverly Hills Hilton. I was in the press room waiting around, and there he was. This man. I'm ogling him, he's ogling me, and after what seemed forever, we're introduced by Mac's publicist, Henri Bollinger. We didn't do much more than have some press pictures taken together, but I sensed that something had happened and hoped he did too. And I guess he did. I was thirty years old, and for a long time I figured I'd turn into the crazy woman down the street with eighteen dogs in the bed and a stack of newspapers so deep you can't find the body. And then I met him. It was simple. Right off the bat I knew.

❝*I had sworn off women when I first met Delta. I'd been married twice and had three kids and felt I'd been a failure as a husband. I had big plans: I was going to go live on my boat and sail around the world. Then I went and fell madly in love with her the first time I saw her. We started to shake hands but hugged each other instead. When I appeared on her show, she invited me into her dressing room, where she had stacks of books. She brought out a book on old plantation homes, because she knew I had grown up around all that stuff. So our first bonding was the South business.*❞ —Gerald McRaney

It was just after Jean's wedding that Mac came onto the set of *DW* to actually work. He was offered a part on one of the first episodes of the second season, playing Dash Goff, the famous writer and my first husband. (My second was a famous baseball player, and the third . . . well, I'm not sure what happened to him.) Mac didn't even ask how long he would work or how much he would get paid. He just said yes. On the set, we kind of circled each other. Mac soon got around to asking me out to lunch, and I'll never forget why I turned him down: I was drinking those damn diet shakes to lose some of my 155 pounds. Now I realize that 155 pounds on me is about right. But around that time everybody really started up with me again about the weight. Once more I began messing with my metabolism to please *them*.

❝*I didn't see Delta after our first meeting for several months. I didn't want her to think I was interested in some fly-by-night romance. But when I came onto the set of* Designing Women*, we had that same immediate attraction. So after our first date, I*

5
9

called the Tuluca Lake florist and had them send her a big bunch of white roses. I had never seen anything that pretty. I included a note, and it said:

'In Mississippi there is a section of the state studded with antebellum homes rich in both beauty and substance. It is so fertile that if one simply casts seeds onto the soil, they sprout and flourish and bring new life. And this enchanted place we call the Delta.' 99 —Gerald McRaney

Needless to say, I was gone over this man. He asked me to marry him on our second date. I said yep right away. It was that clear-cut.

On May 28, 1989, Mac and I first married in a big, beautiful wedding at the Biltmore Hotel in Los Angeles. The festivities were big-time grand—this was going to be my only marriage and I wanted to do it up right. The prerehearsal dinner was a big Mexican fiesta in our backyard. I dressed as Carmen Miranda, and Mac and I planted a white rosebush. *People* magazine covered the wedding. My ten bridesmaids wore emerald taffeta, and I came down the aisle in a low-cut silk gown with a train. We had Scottish bagpipes and trumpet fanfares, the works.

The whole thing was a fantasy come true. When we went in to Tiffany's to pick out my engagement ring, I asked to see the big, fat diamonds. The lady at the counter condescendingly let me know that they didn't call them that. But that's what I got—a big, fat four-carat. I felt so *engaged* in that ring.

Our honeymoon was an extended tour of Europe. Mac dined on elaborate multicourse meals and never put on a pound. I shopped—but not enough, because I gained three pounds.

I had lived alone for so long that I was good at entertaining myself, at pulling out my paints and drawing alone for hours. In fact, I need time alone to recharge. It was an adjustment, but Mac and I have managed to do pretty well. Mac is a rock, a

This shot was taken when Mac guest-starred on Designing Women—playing my husband, Dash Goff, the famous writer—— and things really started to heat up between us. Randee St. Nicholas

steadying influence. He's also one of the nicest, most unassuming people I've ever known. He just got back from visiting William Faulkner's house in Oxford, Mississippi, and while visiting Faulkner's grave was upset to see that it had not been kept up. So he got down on his knees and weeded it. He's now helping to raise funds to buy the historic house a dehumidifier; all those books and artifacts will be ruined otherwise. Mac does things like that all the time, but if he didn't tell me about it, no one would ever know. He is a true gentleman from the old school.

I am lucky. With so many other people, I was a mere reflection: I was always trying to figure out how they perceived me and how they wanted me to act. That's a stressful way to live. With Mac, I didn't have to do that. I could be myself—what a relief! It was the first time that somebody loved me *for me,* not for what I looked like. With Mac, it was safe to be me.

Mac's romantic surprise six-month anniversary dinner in the Biltmore ballroom. Collection of Delta Burke

66 *I still think she's about the most beautiful creature God ever put on this earth.* **99** —Gerald McRaney

The irony is that, having found someone I wanted to be with, we were forced by our production schedules to spend too much time apart. We try to talk every night that we're apart. Mac is a big romantic: He surprised me for our six-month wedding anniversary with a private dinner for two in the same Biltmore ballroom that we were married in. He had musicians and champagne and waiters hovering. Attention of this kind is something I handle very well. These days, I wish we could have more solid chunks of time together, but we always seem to be going in different directions, off to some location or another. It's a typical show-biz marriage in the worst way. Nothing is quite constant in our life, except maybe chaos. But we've still got a nice little love story percolating here. In fact, recently while visiting him on location, my husband said my body is a work of art (bless him!). I didn't bother to ask if he was referring to Impressionist art or Picasso's Blue Period. I took it as a high compliment and like to think of myself as a Botticelli babe.

Our House

Mac and I found a 1920s house in Pasadena that we fell in love with. Actually, it was pretty grand—the house of my dreams—so I guess you could call it a mansion. Let me tell you a little bit about that house. It was full of all sorts of different environments. We had a Florida Room. We had Mac's Hunting Room. We had Delta's Doll Room, to hold my collection. Bookshelves, filled to bursting, ran up and down the walls of several rooms. Off the kitchen, we had a room for our dogs, with bunk beds that they actually slept in. I thought so much of a Memphis artist's work that I invited him to come to Pasadena and paint some walls. He ended up living there, eating Thanksgiving dinner with us, painting more walls and creating decorative wallpaper.

I still think of that house and all it stood for. It was the culmination of my dreams and probably the grandest house I'll

The dogs' bunk beds in Pasadena. Collection of Delta Burke

ever own. It was a real movie star house, and as such was one of the perks of fame. As the stresses mounted in my life, I began to think I'd made a Faustian pact.

Two Emmy Nominations and an Old-Fashioned Nervous Breakdown

You hear about the "pressures of fame" and you think, Oh, come on—you're living in that house making that money married to that man? But for me, trying to please everybody, adjusting to being famous, and the general stress on the set of a hit show that had to keep on being a hit—all this was pushing me past my limits. I wasn't used to finding people hiding out in my shrubbery. Mac was wonderful, but our schedules were crazy. I worked late; he was on the road a lot. My costars on the set were relieved when I got married, because it kind of put the brakes on my workaholic drive, but as *Designing Women* got bigger, the pressures to keep up the momentum mounted.

At the same time, I was trying to become more comfortable with my body. Mac was always supportive, and that made me relax more. I slowly stopped going on starvation diets—and if that meant never being a size 6 again, so be it. But the press decided to make an issue of it—you would have thought I had committed murder. All of a sudden I was the poster girl for large-size women. Some people were unbelievably mean. I read where a group of male reporters on a bus en route to a *Designing Women* party made bets on my bra size. And, according to several vintage tabloid headlines from that period:

1. Mac force-fed me, after which he ordered me out of the house for being too fat.
2. I was chasing Annie Potts around the set and hiding in my dressing room.
3. I confessed after trying caramel hunger suppressants that I loved them so much I ate the whole box!
4. I seduced Gerald with a striptease—and it was all my mom's idea! Well, that one *was* sort of true.
5. "Delta to Replace Roseanne!"
6. "Distraught Delta Stuffing Herself!"
7. I was a Russian spy.
8. I kept a pet gator in my bathtub.

I understand that it is human nature to enjoy watching the famous get knocked off their pedestals. I understand that some folks love seeing a pretty woman grow old or heavy. But this was plain mean. All of a sudden, I had another pressure to deal with—adjusting to my weight while the tabloids fed my

65

Ex-aide claims: Delta battled mental

Star was a 'bedridden, pill-popping blob'

Delta Burke is poised to make a fantastic Hollywood comeback this fall in her new TV comedy "Delta" — but to make it back she had to fight a secret battle against mental illness!

That shocker comes from her former special assistant Amy Coakley. She charges that she helped get Delta back on her feet and even gave her the idea for her new sitcom — only to have Delta repay her by cheating her and having her fired!

In an exclusive ENQUIRER interview, the woman who was Delta's assistant for seven months says that after being fired from "Designing Women," Delta became a self-pitying, bedridden, pill-popping blob without a prospect for a new series.

She also claims the star:

● Stayed in her bedroom for days at a time, eating in bed and filling her house with cheap junk from mail-order catalogs.

● Suffered delusions of grandeur that made her think and act as if she was more important than other people.

● Finally snapped out of it and launched a successful comeback with the help of psychiatric treatment, Amy's pep talks and the controversial depression medication Prozac.

"Delta's new show was my idea," blasted Amy, 36. "Delta was a depressed, bedridden, overweight slob without an idea in her head, and no career ahead of her. I came along, charged her up and gave her a new lease on life. She used me and then dumped me."

Despite repeated calls from The ENQUIRER, Delta's spokesperson said she could not comment on Amy's charges.

Amy had been hired in Au...

By ALAN BRAHAM SMITH

ant at Perseverance — the company Universal studios had set up for her.

Incredibly, Amy says she didn't see Delta for the first six weeks and when the actress finally decided to work, it wasn't at the office.

"Delta would summon me to her home and we'd discuss business on the edge of her bed," declared an astonished Amy. "She'd be in her nightclothes, her hair unkempt, when I would arrive at noon.

"She'd eat her lunch right in front of me and not offer me a thing. The maid would pop down the legs of the tray and Delta would eat her meal of Cheez Whiz, bologna, ham and eggs, potato chips, cream puffs, coffee . . . and Diet Coke."

Delta often followed up with a slew of prescribed drugs.

"She was on medication and seeing a psychiatrist," revealed Amy. "Some days she'd put as many as six pills on a plate right in front of me and she'd ask me to get her a Diet Coke with ice to knock them down. One drug she took regularly was Prozac."

BITTER: Amy Coakley holds photographs of her former boss, Delta Burke. She says

Poor Delta Burke! Marriage to Major Dad hits the rocks when she falls off her diet

Star — October 10, 1989 — 79¢

SHE'S TOO FAT FOR ME, HE BEEFS AFTER ONLY FOUR MONTHS

SISTER KATE'S STEPHANIE BEACHAM, 42, TO MARRY TOY BOY, 32

EXCLUSIVE INTERVIEW

LIZ
How I juggle the two men in

Designing Women's

Top: _National Enquirer_.

Bottom: _Star_.

illness— & won!

she started working for Delta, the star pulled herself out of bed to address a group of 40 influential industry women at the Walt Disney Studio — and stunned them by admitting her mental problems publicly.

"She spilled her guts about a nervous breakdown she had on 'Designing Women,' and what pills she was on," confided Amy. "Everyone, including me,

'I have no reason to get out of bed, no reason to live. I don't want to see anybody'

was in shock." In addition to taking antidepressant drugs like Prozac, Delta seemed to suffer from delusions of grandeur, charged Amy.

When Delta did leave her house, the newly dyed blonde often embarrassed herself in front of other celebrities because of her own stardom, declared Amy.

One time, Delta was getting a facial in Beverly Hills when she spotted Bette Midler.

"She ran up to Bette like her long-lost friend, her arms outstretched, and said: 'Bette, it's great to see you.'

"Bette, who had never met

dio execs. "She'd say: 'I have no reason to get out of bed, no reason to live. I don't want to see anybody,'" revealed Amy.

"She'd say to me: 'I don't have my act together.'

"'I'm such a slob.'"

So Amy says she took matters into her own hands. "I finally got so

mad I stormed dow the house and told 'Get your butt out o You're blowing you chance.'"

After much prod Delta met with exec fall, but they still co come up with an ide a show.

In October, Amy her free-lance wi partner Dean I showed Delta the they had come up w their spare time — a singer who go Nashville to beco country star.

Delta and Univ

Top: National Enquirer.
Bottom: Star.

JUNE 13, 1989 75¢

Star

The honeymoon diet that helped Delta Burke lose 30 lbs

HERE COME THE BRIDES!

Matlock star weds preacher

Delta & groom Gerald McRaney

insecurities. And as those insecurities mounted, so did my weight, to about 170 pounds. That fed the tabloids even more. I had become a big, easy target.

I had worked so hard to build up this career.

For a while, I fought it. First I tried to stand up to the critics and was full of bluster. Then I tried to make light of it. But the constant scrutiny and criticism ultimately wore me down. My whole body language changed. I would let my hair hang down over my face. I was all stooped over. I stopped making appearances. I was trying to disappear in some way, trying not to attract any attention and be as small as I could be. I withdrew and covered my script pages with drawings of miserable, unhappy people.

❝ *I thought the whole mess was ludicrous. She was a fragile little girl; she took everything personally. Delta has the best heart of anyone I know, and she's absolutely beautiful with or without the weight. At times I felt helpless. I kept letting her know how much I loved her and how out of line people were being. And that, when you make a stand like she had, you had better be prepared to take some heat.* ❞ —Gerald McRaney

❝ *If you are a beautiful woman who got fat, you are treated not like someone who got overweight, but like someone who has killed schoolbuses full of children.* ❞ —Linda Bloodworth-Thomason

While all this was going on, Mac and I were buying and fixing up that grand house in Pasadena. (Little did I know that the purchase of a house is considered one of the most stressful events in one's life. Just what I needed.) But as the show and I got more successful, it seemed that that house turned on me. It became filled with people who ran things—they ran my bank accounts, drove me from place to place, arranged my schedules, and made my decisions. It happens a lot in Hollywood, where fame isolates people and being on the go

Four generations: It made perfect sense for a baby named Delta to have a grandmother named Ruby May and a great-grandmother named Palestine Delilah.
Collection of Delta Burke

Here with my brother, Jonathan, and sister, Jennifer, as a Santa's elf for the Montgomery Ward store Teen Board. Collection of Delta Burke

A pink Christmas. Mother let me pick out the Christmas tree that year. I got one in my favorite color and decorated it with pink ornaments. Collection of Delta Burke

Stardust in her eyes:
being introduced as one of
the Tupperware Jubilee's
Constellation of Stars
on the road in Canada.
Tupperware Collection,
Smithsonian Institution,
Washington, D.C.

TUPPERWARE
CONSTELLATION OF STARS

Demurely wearing that tangerine chiffon dress in vying for
Miss Flame. I have no idea what that fellow in the overalls is
doing. Collection of Delta Burke

As Miss All-Veterans Day 1973, I got to meet the fleet. Notice the sailor's nervous fondling of my white gloves as we chat.
Collection of Delta Burke

I did my duty as Miss Flame.
Orlando Sentinel

When I wasn't competing in pageants, I was throwing myself headlong into acting in Central Florida Civic Theatre productions. Here I was the princess in *Aladdin*.
Civic Theatre of Central Florida, Orlando.
Jack Dunathan

Miss Florida, with proud Mom and Dad.   Ed Stout

Vamping as the newly crowned Miss Orlando 1974. Ed Stout

Clowning around with my Miss Florida robe and scepter. Collection of Delta Burke

Miss Florida and Miss Georgia on the
Atlantic City boardwalk.
Hess Photography, Atlantic City

Mama added extra
sequins to this already
high-voltage sequined
dress; the result being
I unwittingly out-
flashed the new Miss
Florida. A little is
good, Mom always
says, but more is
better.
Collection of Delta Burke

Polished and madeover in Atlantic City for the
Miss America pageant, with my cousin Kelly,
Jonathan, and Jennifer.   Collection of Delta Burke

Cute and chubby at my going-away-to-London party.
Collection of Delta Burke

The new Delta in London: wild and witchy.
Collection of Delta Burke

Nana, my chaperone, and me on the set of
Charleston.   Collection of Delta Burke

I got to wear lots of fun clothes on
The Love Boat.
Collection of Delta Burke

Fresh-faced in Hollywood. One of my earliest photos in Hollywood.
Collection of Delta Burke

Haughty and oversexed on the set of <u>Remington Steele</u>. Pierce Brosnan was the nicest, most down-to-earth guy.
Collection of Delta Burke

Stacy Keach helped me raise my acting to a new level when I guest-starred on <u>Mike Hammer</u>. Collection of Delta Burke

The girls celebrate at the wrap party for the Designing Women pilot. From left, Jean Smart, Dixie Carter, me, and Annie Potts.
Collection of Delta Burke

With The Chisholms cast, including Rosemary Harris (with hand on my shoulders). Playing Bonnie Sue Chisholm, I started hearing whisperings about my weight. Photofest (The Chisholms)

A-courtin'. Mac loved this outfit——with a frothy little can-can skirt, a bolero top, and monster earrings——that I wore on my thirty-first birthday.
Collection of Delta Burke

Getting married at the Biltmore Hotel in Los Angeles——a grand affair!
Jonathon Farrer Photography

The third season of _Designing Women_, when I really got grief for my weight gain. (I'm holding Stella for comfort.)
CBS Photo Archives

One of the best-loved episodes from _Designing Women_ featured Anthony, played by Mesach Taylor, and me sharing clothes and bonding in a cold hotel room. Photofest (_DesigningWomen_). Gene Arias

Troubled time. At the start of the third season of Designing Women, I was breaking from all the pressures. I was in tears most of the time for this photo shoot.
CBS Photo Archives

I felt comfortable enough with my body to let People magazine photograph me in my birthday suit as one of the Most Fascinating People of 1990.
Douglas Kirkland/Sygma

In Nashville at the Grand Ole Opry, doing research for my new show called Delta.

Photofest (*Delta*).
Bob D'Amico

I was at my heaviest weight when I made Day-O, a TV movie with the wonderful, talented Elijah Wood. Photofest (*Day-O*)

I met a lot of great country-music stars doing the sitcom _Delta_. They included the fabulous _Loretta Lynn_ (my dog Loretta's namesake) and ultra-talented _Trisha Yearwood_ (below).

Photos collection of Delta Burke

A great show and Suzanne Sugarbaker's swan song: <u>Women of the House</u>.
Photofest (*Women of the House*)

I'm a crown magnet—people always bring me their crowns. Here a local drag queen (an impersonation of me is in his repertoire) brings me his tiara at a personal appearance for Delta Burke Design. Collection of Delta Burke

leaves little time for the realities of day-to-day life. Eventually people come in and say, "I'm going to take care of you and make everything work so you can go and be famous." You want to believe them. You want to believe that they are interested in taking care of you. So the next thing you know, you can't even get yourself a glass of water. I didn't know what I had, I didn't know what I owed, I wasn't seeing my family. I was like a domesticated animal in a way, a trick pony. They'd prop me up on stage and I'd go into my act. I became even more isolated because of the weight situation, and before I knew it, I had relinquished control of my life and didn't even know it. With all the success came not more control, but less.

The Show That Made History: "They Shoot Fat Women, Don't They?"

My coping skills prior to *Designing Women* had basically consisted of shutting down and recharging when filming was over. I couldn't do that on a weekly sitcom. It was weird; I'd be a complete mess off the set, but the minute I hit the stage I was fine—It was as if I was home.

But there was no question that I was breaking down. I had been trying so hard to be perfect, but I never felt good enough. I didn't understand why everyone had gotten so ugly. And I was trying to handle being famous and the constant invasions into my privacy. I had worked so hard for this moment, but it was like getting all my dreams answered with a price.

My breakdown occurred at the end of the second season. I started having debilitating panic attacks. By the time I was finally hospitalized for that famous Hollywood condition "nervous exhaustion," I hated myself and wanted to die. The nurse who admitted me later said I looked like a wounded animal.

The hospitalization gave me a safe place to go. With therapy, medication, and coping skills to short-circuit the panic attacks, I made it back to the *Designing Women* set for the third season. A big part of my therapy was learning to say no. The old Delta, out there on the stump, making every appearance and every ribbon cutting, simply could not continue and at the same time do good creative work and stay sane.

I don't understand the stigma about therapy. Everyone at some time or another faces some sort of crisis for which he or she needs help. It certainly has brought me a long way. But other factors contributed to my getting stronger. A women's self-defense class was offered that year on the set, and I took it along with a lot of the female crew. The woman who was teaching it was very large, and yet she was free and open with her body. She appeared strong, empowered, and best of all, not embarrassed. Seeing that inspired me. All of a sudden it was me getting up there and being physically powerful and not hiding.

Linda Bloodworth-Thomason had always been keyed in to my emotional state—you can track my own personal growth through Suzanne's. But in all that time I don't recall Linda ever giving me any grief about my weight. In fact, I don't recall her ever saying anything about it. It was just not an issue for her.

So I went to her prior to our fourth season and said I wanted to do a show about the weight. Linda admitted that she hadn't dealt with the weight issue because she wasn't sure how *I* was going to deal with it, whether I was going to lose the weight or stay that way. I told her I'd like to lose it but it didn't look like that was going to happen—but we had to deal with it. And I said, "Please let me have the jokes about the weight, rather than be the butt of the jokes. Give me the power." It was a way to take control of the issue, no more "let's pretend it's not there." It was like having a huge hump on your back and everyone saying, "What hump?"

So Linda went and wrote this beautiful script, "They Shoot Fat Women, Don't They?" It was all about Suzanne Sugarbaker going to a class reunion and being stung by catty comments about her weight from old classmates. In one scene Suzanne escapes to the ladies' room, only to overhear a former classmate describe her as "the new poster girl for Save the Whales." Another classmate jokes that the reason Suzanne's three husbands left her is that "they weren't getting enough to eat." Suzanne is devastated.

❝ Doing that show was very important to her. Had it not been in her hands—I felt the script was a little maudlin in places—it may not have worked. But she knocked it out of the park. ❞

—Linda Bloodworth-Thomason

When I showed the script to Mac, he cried. He called Linda and thanked her for "writing such a wonderful script for my baby." The day of the taping was a very emotional one. I could sense a shift in everyone; it was like one great big sigh of relief. In the final scene, the reunion awards dinner, Suzanne is "honored" as the "Person Most Changed." The thank-you speech she gives is a killer—and as close to the bone as anything I have ever done.

Well, this is quite a surprise. I guess I deserve this award for the person most changed but not for the reasons you think.

Last night I got my feelings hurt, because I came to this reunion thinking I was beautiful—and what I found out was that I'm fat. At least you think I am.

But that isn't the biggest change in me. The biggest change is that the old Suzanne wouldn't have shown up here tonight. She would have gotten thin for the next reunion, and then she would have gotten even.

But I'm a little older and, I hope, a little wiser than that person used to be. A lot of things have happened to me. A lot of things have happened to others. Sandy Smothers was killed the night before we graduated. Diane Mitchell's got two sets of twins, and Galin Chadwicks's working in the White House. We had a lot of dreams together. And there's no point pretending. Some of mine came true—and some didn't.

7
1

I met a little boy from Africa tonight whose family died of starvation, and I realized that I spent the whole day worrying about having too much to eat. I'm not sure the old Suzanne would have appreciated the absurdity of that—but this one does.

Some of you men wanted to know my bra size, but I'd rather talk about my heart because—it's a little bigger than it used to be.

The old Suzanne wouldn't have forgiven you for the things you said, but this one will, because when I look around this room tonight, I don't see receding hairlines or the beginnings of pot bellies and crows' feet.

I just see all the beautiful faces of old girlfriends, and sweet young boys who used to stand on my front porch and try and kiss me good night. And you can remember me any way you'd like, but that's how I'll remember you.

So I thank you for giving me this award for the person most changed, however you intended it. I'm gonna treasure it, because, number one, I love trophies, and number two, I earned it. Thank you.

The audience gave the cast a standing ovation. I hugged Linda and thanked her.

I felt empowered. It felt as if my body was freed. Instead of trying to hide and cover up and move as little as possible, I got my physical comedy skills back. And once the weight was discussed out in the open on the show, it relieved a lot of the overall stress for everyone else. I could even see the crew lighten up.

In turn, the character of Suzanne became empowered. It wasn't other people making fun of Suzanne. Suzanne made the jokes. With great lines like:

I'll admit I have put on a few pounds here and there, but you all act like I should be ordering fabric from Georgia Tent & Awning!

Or, leaving in a huff when Julia agrees that Suzanne *has* put on some weight and that she may not be able to cover it up at the class reunion and that she just doesn't want Suzanne to get her feelings hurt:

I'll just be going now—if you think the streets of Atlanta can stand the strain of both me and my Mercedes! Or maybe I should just have one of those big trucks drive in front of me, you know, warning people, with a sign that says: Caution: Wide Load.

"They Shoot Fat Women, Don't They?" was the turn-around. It was the beginning of my reclaiming myself.

The funny thing is, the character got more interesting and complex the heavier I got. Her personal liberation was born with Linda's words. Suzanne started out as a one-dimensional beauty queen who felt she was God's gift to man. When the weight came on, I found I couldn't hide her behind a camera angle or a clever A-line skirt. With the weight, Suzanne developed an emotional depth. I had to portray a beautiful ex–beauty queen at a time when I never felt farther from being one. It made me dig deeper and tap into my skills. So the character acquired depth and shading. She became so much richer—she became this *great broad.* And you know what? She never stopped believing she was beautiful. She would still strut across the room. She got sassier. She held her head high.

After the show aired, the letters of support were overwhelming. Oprah Winfrey sent a telegram saying that she would never forget the line, "All that counts is what was true, and truly felt. And how we treated one another." That show, and all the wonderful things that came along with it, truly was the beginning of the person I am now.

❝ Before the show, I went to Delta on an almost daily basis and told her how little I cared about her weight. A woman asking another woman to lose weight—that is simply not something I would do! I told her that as long as she was funny, she could be any weight she wanted. In fact, I thought Suzanne

became a more interesting character with the weight and more fun to write for. "" —Linda Bloodworth-Thomason

The Blonde in the Classroom, Part II

My seasons with *Designing Women* went something like this: The first season was a rocket ride; the second season I was stressed and exhausted; the third season was when the character really began to take off and become multidimensional. It was no coincidence that this occurred simultaneously with my weight gain. The fourth season I was much more together; it was the year of "Fat Women," and I was nominated for an Emmy (and, oh, what to wear!). I was so damn excited. My family all came to the awards show, including my uncle Jimmy, and I designed the dress I wore. I lost out to the wonderfully talented Candice Bergen, but I really think I did my best work that year.

By the fifth season, I was much more easygoing about everything. I had learned, through intensive and difficult therapy, that there were, there are, and there will be some things I had simply to let go of. I felt strong enough to go public with the weight situation, which made me feel even more comfortable with myself. Instead of trying to hide and show my body as little as possible, I started flaunting my body. I was once more nominated for an Emmy, but I felt my performances were not as strong as they were the year before. Still, if the voters were in a *Butterfield 8* mood, I wasn't going to turn it down. Not to worry: I lost again.

At the same time, the work had become grueling, and after five years and going through lots of emotional changes, Linda and I often found ourselves in conflict. The strange part of all this was that Linda's people were telling my people that we were in conflict, and my people were telling Linda's people we were in conflict, when all that time *Linda and I* should have been talking to each other.

I had been asking to be released from the show since the third season, but all along the producers refused to let me out of my contract. That is, until the end of the fifth season, in 1991, when Mac and I were in New Orleans shooting *Love and Curses and All That Jazz,* a TV movie (where one scene has us staging our marriage in the St. Louis Cathedral). Mac broke the news to me. "Sweetie," he said gently, "they didn't renew your option." My first reaction, a big smile, failed to hide my surprise at finally being let go. Later, of course, the ego kicked in. I started to question why I was fired. I was hurt—I had never been fired from anything, ever! But as time went on, I felt relieved and revitalized, excited about moving forward. I realized that if you don't keep going, they'll get you; if you don't keep on, they'll win.

Although things were better for me emotionally, the end of *Designing Women* was a tough adjustment and a bit of an emotional setback. My insecurities mounted. I had been working like a maniac for nearly twenty years, and, frankly, I was beat. If I took time off, would I ever get work again? Then I was offered the chance to produce my own situation comedy, *Delta.* It was something I had wanted for a long time, and I couldn't turn it down.

At the time, I was still carrying around the character of Suzanne. I'd look in the mirror and *see* Suzanne. And all the painful memories would take over. So I determined I was going to look as drastically different as I could. I had always wanted to go blond, from lessons I learned from the blonde in my first-grade classroom to my grown-up fascination with Marilyn Monroe. So, before I started shooting *Delta* and a television movie called *Day-O* in North Carolina, I asked my hair-stylist in Los Angeles to lighten my hair. I thought it was the kind of thing I needed at the time. I thought the lighter hair would somehow lighten my heart. Because in truth, I was extremely unhappy with how my body looked. I was heavier than I had *ever* been, a size 22 at 215 pounds. So, for all of those reasons, I went blond. It took the stylist three days to transform me from totally brunette to platinum blond.

❝ *When Delta went blond, I knew it wasn't right for her. She has a beautiful, almost Irish complexion that perfectly matches her black hair. But she needed a change to get over her depression. That's the amazing thing about hair, how it can change your attitude about yourself.* ❞ —Virginia Kearns, Hollywood hairstylist

The situation comedy *Delta* was set in a Nashville honky-tonk, and I played a waitress in the bar where Patsy Cline was discovered and an aspiring country music singer. Yes, I *sang.* We always had great country music stars popping in to the bar to play themselves, singers like Tanya Tucker and Trisha Yearwood. To say the show was the polar opposite of everything Suzanne was would be putting it mildly. Unfortunately, the reviews were a departure as well.

❝ *Delta Builds Early Lead as Worst New TV Series.* ❞

—Headline, *Montreal Gazette*

Many of the reviews concentrated more on my weight than the show's shortcomings. The message was: Look how far Delta has fallen; *how sad.*

I worked hard to make that series work, but I didn't have much fight in me at that point. Because to create a successful television show, you have to roll with the punches. I saw how hard Linda and Harry had to fight on *Designing Women* and *Women of the House.* And I decided I just didn't need the heartache.

Toward the end of the show, I abandoned my blond hair. Once again, I had been trying to transform myself into that pretty little blonde in the classroom who got all the attention and fussing over. Trying to please everyone. Always running away from myself. It was time to find the real me.

If You Don't Keep Going, They'll Get You!

I started 1995 by taking my first time off in twenty-odd years. I wasn't even sure whether I wanted to keep acting or not. I knew I wasn't tough enough yet to deal with the constant rejection. I've always been trusting of people, and people have not always responded in kind. On the other hand, I kind of like the fact that I survived fifteen years in Hollywood without becoming completely cynical. I give a lot of credit to the people who raised me.

So out of the blue, my agent, Marty Hurwitz, calls and says, "You'll never guess who wants to work with you again." It turned out that Linda Bloodworth-Thomason wanted me to reprise my role as Suzanne Sugarbaker in a new situation comedy that was created for me. The show was to be set in

Here I am with Dolly Parton while making an appearance with her at "Dollywood." Collection of Delta Burke

Washington, D.C., where Suzanne is appointed to take over her late (fifth) husband's seat in Congress.

Women of the House, like *Designing Women,* was beautifully written. Linda had a fine time getting in a few jabs at some of the Washington crowd who were so hard on her and Harry and their relationship with the Clintons. Here's a piece of work that is pure Linda, put into the sassy speech of United States Representative Suzanne Sugarbaker, in her maiden speech to Congress:

I've been told that Washington is a place where you have to fit in. Well I'm a person who likes to stand out. Now I've said a lot of things this week that are politically incorrect, but then, so am I. My maid is black. My daughter is adopted. My brother is retarded. And I myself am five times married, fat—not "zaftig"—big-mouthed, Southern and rich. Newly rich, which, if you ask me, is the best kind to be, because it means you earned it yourself. . . . In Washington, anyone who doesn't wear support hose is flamboyant. . . . But being different is what America's about. . . . It's about people who like to dust, who drink too much, people with cleavage.

It was a good show and a good cast and crew. I was consulted on scripts and felt like part of the creative team. We got great reviews.

❝*A win—a deliciously nasty culture clash.*❞

—Harry Waters, *Newsweek*

❝*A clown of renown, Burke is never funnier than when playing Suzanne Sugarbaker.*❞ —Matt Roush, *USA Today*

❝*Hilarious . . . Burke is a brilliant, feisty, tremendously appealing comedienne*❞ —Liz Smith, syndicated columnist

❝ *Full of snap and crackle and great humor writing—Burke is simply ravishing.* **❞** —Julia Keller, *Columbus Dispatch*

God! It was so *great* to finally have something nice said about me and my work. And this show truly deserved a better shot than it got and so did the cast—Teri Garr, Patricia Heaton, Valerie Mahaffey, and dear, sweet Jonathan Banks as my brother. Such talent! I learned a great deal from them. (I also loved sneaking next door to hang out with John Ritter and Billy Bob Thornton on their *Hearts Afire* set. Hot damn but those are some flat-out funny folks.) But I digress. Doing a weekly sitcom was still stressful; that's the nature of the work. But in spite of the stress, the show was a success. Most important, Linda and I found our friendship again, allowing everything to come full circle. Besides getting good reviews, *Women of the House* served a purpose of closure for Linda and me. Reaching out for me was an extraordinarily generous gesture on Linda's part, and I am happy to have a dear friend back. Yet when *Women of the House* was canceled, I knew it was time to move on. So I said good-bye to Linda and a familiar way of working. My work with her had been the most rewarding and creative of my life. But most of all, it was time to part ways with that big, brassy ex–beauty queen from Atlanta. Suzanne and I had done a lot of growing up together.

The Designing Woman

My growing feeling of well-being was reflected in my physical attitude. Although my interest in clothes had never waned, my enthusiasm for stylish dressing returned with a vengeance. I felt good, damn it, and I wanted to look good! But I found it next to impossible to find smart-looking, well-made clothes. There was little to be found with any sort of flair or construction fit. It was futile looking for sexy evening wear, lingerie, or swimsuits. Styles came in two colors and were stuck down in dingy store basements, which only reinforced a sense of shame for being big. The mind-set was that if you get to a certain size,

Big, bright, and happy at Mardi Gras in New Orleans.
Collection of Delta Burke

you automatically aren't a real person anymore. You aren't a sexual person anymore. Just hang it up and throw on that big black Hefty bag.

But I refused to wear those frumpy old clothes. At the time of my very publicized weight gain, I was working on the set of *Designing Women,* so I asked the show's designer, Cliff Chally, to create clothes for Suzanne that were sexy and wearable. It was really a collaboration: I have always designed clothes, coming by it naturally, of course, from my mother. I designed both my wedding gowns. On locations, I doodle away, drawing outfits and costumes and what I call my pretty ladies.

The clothes we created suited me. Cliff made pretty peplum jackets that flared at the bottom and jewel-neck dresses in electric colors. In the years that followed, I learned even more: how to use fabric, how to find a comfortable fit, how to adapt to new styles. Pretty soon, I was making best-dressed lists all over the country. Suddenly, the notion of designing my own collection of clothes took on a life of its own; in fact, I was approached several times by several different companies to do just that. It was simply a matter of waiting for the right group of people, people who shared my philosophy.

With Delta Burke Design, I found a dynamic, committed team to dress my real-size ladies. The Delta Burke lifestyle collection was launched in 1994 and now has licenses for jeanswear, lingerie, activewear, soft dressing, evening wear, and swimsuits. I have plus-size patterns with Butterick. I'm not just a celebrity name; I'm totally involved. My ideas for designs come from old movies and movie stills from the 1940s and 1950s, when fit and construction were unmatched. I get inspiration from museums and costume exhibits. Whenever I'm in a new city, I seek out the antiques shop and buy old postcards with Victorian lithographs or prints. I also help select fabric and conduct fit sessions. But most important, I wear the clothes.

With Delta Burke Design, I can share all I've learned about clothing with other real-size ladies. My mandate is to provide options in dressing and style, options that I was privileged to be exposed to. But there is so much more I have to share. In the next few chapters, I'll give you all my secrets on dressing, makeup, skin care, hair styling, attitude, and shopping. Just follow me.

CHAPTER 2

Why Weight?

66 *Between the rumors about her professional, marital, and weight problems, Delta has received more mention in the tabloids than Elvis Presley's ghost.* 99

—Barbara Walters, introduction to interview with Delta in 1990

Beauty as Currency

I'll admit: I was spoiled by the press coverage I got in my beauty pageant days. I was "Snow White" with the

"Barbie-doll figure." I was treated equally well by the local media in Hollywood during my first few years there. Okay, they thought I was a little nutty at times, but generally interviewers lobbed puffballs in my direction and just sat back and let me be me.

My honeymoon with the press came to an end, however, once I put on weight. I went from being Barbie on a pedestal to a sexless, unattractive nonentity. Imagine that—I was thirty-two years old and no longer considered a sexual being. Well, *really*: Who would be interested in a big old dumpling like me?

Whereas my husband, who is balding, who is getting a little bit of a potbelly, and who is now fifty, nonetheless is expected to romance twenty-year-olds in his on-screen roles. He is not alone. Dennis Franz, the Emmy Award–winning actor on *NYPD Blue,* was *asked* to bare his butt in a love scene for the show. Now don't get me wrong. I think Dennis is adorable and sexy— but he's hardly a slim, buff model type out of the pages of *GQ.* You don't see many women in less than perfect shape and of a certain age doing romantic love scenes in their birthday suits. Even perfect is not good enough if you're a woman: Body doubles sub for many of the most beautiful young actresses in Hollywood in nude scenes. Not that I would ever want to bare my own butt on film, but they wouldn't even *ask* me.

Then there's John Goodman, formerly of *Roseanne,* who not so long ago was named one of the "10 Sexiest Men Alive" by *People* magazine. John *is* sexy, John *is* adorable. But he's a great-big, real-size guy! No *woman* of an equivalent size would even be considered for such an accolade.

It's been said that discrimination against overweight people is the last accepted prejudice. Now that science has proved that weight is often genetically determined, we know that some people will never be a size 6 without compromising their health and well-being. But for women, much more so than men, the stereotypes and the discrimination persist, helped along by society's kiss of approval.

Maybe that's because women are still judged more on their appearance than on their abilities. Which means that ladies of size are often treated like second-class citizens. I've heard some horror stories you would not believe. I've heard of women who've had food snatched out of their shopping carts and been told, "You don't need that!" Even those who are well-meaning—especially the naturally slender—can be tactless, gently advising real-size friends who reach for the sugar packet at restaurants to "use the sugar substitute instead." Why, I've known women who have been *mooed* at. One high school student asked his real-size classmate if she was descended from Sumo wrestlers. Another lady of size attended a dance party and had not been asked to dance all night until a man who seemed friendly and genuine swept her onto the floor. She later discovered that she had been the object of a practical joke: His buddies had bet him a hundred dollars to dance with her.

Cruel beyond belief. We fight this issue all the time in the film business. I can't name one famous real-size woman who consistently plays a romantic lead. When it does happen, the pairing is labeled "offbeat" or the relationship "a departure from the norm." It has a sort of freak-show appeal, and if the actress is at all successful, it's always *in spite of* her weight. But in the movies, paunchy fifty-plus men ride off with the money and the girl—and I do emphasize *girl*.

We women are coconspirators, buying into all that "ideal image" stuff. It seems that image has become more important than reality. I know—I was always battling to attain a fantasy image.

Just because you win pageants, and you know people think that you're pretty, doesn't mean *you* think you're pretty. I've known few beautiful women who thought that they were beautiful, who could appreciate themselves—because if that is your only value in life, your only currency, then you can never be beautiful enough.

For a long time I thought my looks were my only currency,

and when that was gone, what would be left? In a wonderful scene from *Designing Women*, written by Linda Bloodworth-Thomason, Suzanne Sugarbaker is lamenting to her sister Julia that her struggle with weight has been lifelong and that people have always been trying to make her into something she's not. The scene speaks volumes about the shame that real-size women are made to feel.

SUZANNE: The point is, [being overweight] is different for women, especially beautiful women. Look at Elizabeth Taylor. . . . All of a sudden, because she got fat, it was like—she no longer had the right to live in this country. And that's how I feel right now. Boy: drugs, alcohol, cancer—whatever your problems, people are sympathetic, unless you're fat. And then you're supposed to be ashamed. Everything's set up to tell you that—magazine covers, clothes—I mean, if you're not thin, you're not neat. And that's it. And if looks are all you've ever had . . .

Julia Sugarbaker, played by Dixie Carter, gives a wonderfully indignant rebuttal:

JULIA: Wait a minute. What do you mean "if looks are all you've ever had"? Suzanne, first of all, don't be a dummy. Your looks will never be in the past tense. That face speaks for itself, and it's here to stay.

Secondly, even if that weren't so, who cares? In the end, it doesn't matter what anybody else thinks about you. People gonna forget you about ten minutes after you die anyway.

The point is, you have to be exactly who and what you want to be. Most everybody's coasting on phony public relations. People who say being beautiful or rich or thin makes them happy, people who are trying to make their marriage or their children seem better than they are—and for what? Appearances! Appearances don't count for diddly. When it's all said and done, all that counts is what was true, and truly felt. And how we treated one another. And that's it.

 Amen.

The Battle for Fashion Equality

Some people would argue that beauty pageants, in promoting an impossible ideal, are part of the problem. For me, at the time, there was no other outlet. I wasn't good at sports, I had few hobbies. In fact, there weren't the kinds of options available for women that are out there today in sports, in business, in any number of professions. Glass ceilings weren't even an issue—it was hard to get your big toe in through the front

Even as a teen—here spoofing beauty queens in a blond wig—I knew that pageants were simply a means to an end. Collection of Delta Burke

door. Pageants were my ticket out. What started as a fun family hobby helped me boost my self-esteem and communicate more comfortably.

Today the choices for women have greatly increased, but we are still being bombarded with images that are impossible to live up to. Not to mention the real-life hurdles we face

Size 6 and starving in a Hollywood kitchen. Collection of Delta Burke

daily: ordinary issues such as comfortable theater seats, decent-size hospital gowns, and airline seat belts we can fit into. Why should we be made to feel embarrassed at every turn?

The perception of fat people is that they eat too much, that their fat is a result of overindulgence and laziness. For many of us, this is a fallacy. My dieting was sheer punishment: The only way I could keep relatively thin was not to eat at all. "Overindulging" meant having an extra twenty-calorie cracker.

Thin is an obsession these days, which makes dieting big business. In the United States alone, it is said that more than 150,000 anorectics die every year from not eating—and many anorectics have suffered from eating disorders from the time they were only eight years old! Even harder to believe: The National Institute of Compulsive Eating reports that 80 percent of ten-year-old girls have been on some kind of diet. What kind of intense pressure are we putting on children these days that forces them to fear basic sustenance?

We can't escape the images—they come at us from all directions: magazines, billboards, television shows. I can't even look at a bus stop these days without feeling a sense of inadequacy. Advertisers show an incredibly thin, fantastically beautiful woman and whisper in your ear, "Here's the way to become the fantasy." What they don't tell you is that the thin, beautiful woman on the billboard is in fact a physical curiosity—generally six inches taller and thirty pounds lighter than the average teenage girl—and any imperfections are airbrushed away. But her image reigns as the icon of the beauty industry, selling millions of dollars' worth of clothes and makeup and diet drinks and cellulite creams. And consumers buy the newest diet product, and young girls skip meals, and the whole process rolls along.

It seems to me that we in the entertainment business and society as a whole have a responsibility to show our daughters and sisters that a world full of options is theirs for the picking.

We need to teach them they need not compromise themselves in unhappy or unhealthy ways in order to meet an idealized image. We have to show these girls that there are many definitions of beauty, so they don't feel compelled to chase down an image that, for a sizable segment of the population, is murder-

Young and clueless at sixteen. Collection of Delta Burke

ous to maintain. We have to free young girls from the rules and constraints set by commercial image makers and give them some breathing room to let their own, unique beauty evolve from the inside out. It's time to balance the scales of beauty justice. It's time for a little fashion equality.

" Many of us have developed an inner rating system that is based on idealized images that we could never hope to live up to. . . . Perhaps the most tragic thing that can happen to us is that we separate ourselves from our own emotions in order to please others, and we go through life pretending to be someone we're not. Image becomes so real that we aren't even sure we are in there. Don't let impossible standards ruin your life. Don't wait until you lose 20 or 30 or 40 pounds to recognize your essential beauty. Recognize your beauty today! "

—Jane Claypool, *Wise Women Don't Worry, Wise Women Don't Sing the Blues*

Making Changes

My life changed considerably when I moved to New Orleans. When I'm home now, I'm really *home.* Some people thought I was nuts to leave Los Angeles—that's where the "work" was, the only work that mattered. But following your heart is a concept I believe many women can understand. Take Marcia Clark, for example. The L.A. prosecutor might never have made the headlines for the O. J. Simpson criminal trial if several years ago she hadn't given up a promotion to a supervisory position to stick to the work she loved—being a trial attorney. Would a man have done that? Hard to say. Or take Audrey Hepburn, who turned her back on the movies at the height of her film career to semiretire to Italy and raise her young son. Plus, I still don't get the brouhaha made just last year over Sherry Stringfield's decision to leave the number-one television show *E.R.* to move to New York and live a less public life with her then-boyfriend. Seems as if she too was stunned—she was sure there were other people out there besides herself who didn't think the pinnacle of success was fame. She was sure there were other people who didn't want their faces splashed all over magazine covers, who cherished their privacy.

It has taken me twenty-five years of living in the public eye to come to the realization that the things that make me happy are not necessarily what other people think should make me happy. And they're not even the things I thought I wanted. Today, at forty-one, I am dealing with a different emotional and physical me.

❝ When Delta came to see me, she didn't trust herself to identify her own feelings and act on them. I find in my practice that this applies to many women, in all walks of life. It has to do with the social roles prescribed to them. Women have not been trained to trust their own judgment. It's ironic, because their instincts are usually right on; many just don't have the confidence to act on them. ❞ —Dr. Dennis Cabe

When I was working so hard to stay thin, what I thought and felt seemed much less important to others than how I looked. But after I gained weight, an amazing thing happened: When I talked, people actually listened. What I said had meaning! This made me feel empowered and enriched, which in turn fed my emotional and intellectual growth. Now I revel in the wealth I have within me. For the first time in my life, I don't feel at the mercy of other people or their expectations. My mistakes and my successes are my own, and I take full responsibility for them. That's why I believe that many good things came along with the weight. I went through pain and humiliation but came out of it happier, stronger, more alive. I've learned to accept—and celebrate—the woman I am.

The trick, I now believe, is, *Don't give other people the power to determine how you live your life.* That power belongs to you. Learn to stop internalizing the negative voices, the ones that say "You can't wear this" or "You're too fat for that." In other words, if you feel strongly about something, go with your instincts. Solicit other people's advice, get second opinions, but make your own decisions regarding the important things. Finally, don't put off living because someone else has decided that you aren't entitled, that you don't measure up, that you don't fit an image. Take control of your own life today, and *start living!*

Body Language: Working It!

Even in my early days in Hollywood, costumers had to find bombshell clothes to fit me. That was fine by me, because I had always loved Marilyn Monroe and her kind of curves. When I posed for pictures, I spoofed the old Marilyn/Varga girl poses from the 1940s and 1950s. From them I learned to play up my naturally curvy shape.

At the same time, I was conscious of the behind-the-scenes

A reporter once called me "a combination of Fanny Brice and a Playboy bunny." Here I am mimicking the over-the-top Varga girl poses while making the TV movie A Bunny's Tale. Collection of Delta Burke

whispering regarding my body's imperfections. My hips were too big, my thighs too chunky—light her this way, dress her that way. Comments like that were not the most pleasant things to hear, so I did the only thing I knew to do: Have fun with it, spoof it. I shut myself down emotionally and kept it all on a light note. I made everything about myself—hair, makeup, poses—oversize and over the top. They weren't going to make fun of me. By god, I'd do it first!

I also caught on to certain tricks and illusions to fool the camera. For example, I learned "the line"—posing in that sexy Varga girl way, with one leg in front of the other, to make my legs look slimmer.

After I was dropped from *Designing Women,* I was contractually required to come back to the set and shoot some promotional spots for syndication. It felt so weird to be back on that stage, but I worked hard to appear upbeat, to let everyone know that I was handling being back on the set with ease.

I was a blonde at the time, so I needed to wear a wig to shoot the promos. It was when I put on the "Suzanne" wig, that big-haired, sassy-broad hairdo, that all the old feelings flooded in. The feelings of being under attack and all alone, of being in emotional distress. Putting on that wig sent me zooming back to that unhappy, painful time, and I was overwhelmed with sadness. Doing those promos was probably the hardest acting job I've ever done.

Like Dorothy in *The Wizard of Oz,* all along I had within me the tools to turn a bad experience into a positive one. When I was working on the situation comedy *Filthy Rich,* my role as the bombshell bimbo widow of the family patriarch made me an easy target, and I was always being put down and made fun of by the other characters. Being a bit sensitive, I sometimes took "the abuse" personally. Because I was given few opportunities to make snappy comebacks, I learned to use my body to do the talking. I learned to flip my hair with my hand, tip my chin up, walk a sassy walk. Put a prop in my hand and get out of the way!

After a long period of being miserable from the down-and-dirty brouhaha over my weight, I finally reached the point where I knew: *I just cannot be that thin, I cannot starve myself anymore, I will not starve myself anymore.* That meant I was going to have to *make it work for me.* So that's when I started to flaunt it.

Today, when I do personal appearances for my clothing line, I do a lot of looking at *you* and how plain old body language can convey an upbeat attitude and confidence—as well as the opposite. I've seen some ladies, size 14 and completely beautiful,

Silent expression, I learned ways to use body language in my work.

Randee St. Nicholas

all slumped over, eyes down, and dragging their feet. Then in struts another beautiful lady, a size 22 or 24, but little attention is paid her size. She's walking tall and glowing—and comes across as fiercely confident and proud. She's flaunting it all over the place, and the result is a thing of beauty.

Every now and then remind yourself to project with your walk, posture, and language. Use what you have—don't try to hide it. Soon that confidence will become second nature.

A few tips on body language:

- Make eye contact. Lock in to whomever you're talking with.
- Walk into a room with back straight and chest out but relaxed, not stiff.
- Hands on hips is a sign of confidence.
- Hold your head high to signal pride and strength.
- Smile when you meet someone and give a firm hand-shake. There's nothing worse than being greeted with a "wet fish" shake.
- Find a comfortable posture. My grandmother used to tell me that by shrugging my shoulders and letting them fall, they fell into my natural posture. Try it.

❝ Delta is one hundred percent girl. She loves high heels. She loves bubble baths. She loves perfume. As her body changed, she never stopped being feminine—with Delta it was inbred. And she came to the realization that size has absolutely nothing to do with femininity. ❞

—Cassandra Scott, skin care specialist and makeup artist

Body language is only part of it. A sense of humor is a real atti-tude adjuster. On *Designing Women,* I was finally able to turn the tables on the gossips by getting to the fat jokes first. In real life, a sense of humor has gotten me through a lot. It's gotten me through "How fat are you?" and "Oh, you're the fat one, right?" It's not easy; I'm constantly struggling with it. But I've learned not to give others the pleasure of pushing my buttons. Sometimes the rudeness is so absurd you have to laugh at it.

It's not as if I have to tell myself jokes to cheer up. Funny things seem to happen to me all the time. For Mac's fortieth birthday, for example, I got him a big cake, gave him gifts that covered all his hobbies, and generally fussed over him. What was left but to turn myself into a giant gift? During our little celebration with a few family members, I had my mother keep Mac occupied while I disappeared upstairs. Then I yelled downstairs to Mom to send him up! *Very* romantic. When Mac came in, there I was, striking a pose and wearing nothing but hot-pink gift ribbons placed in strategic locations. The bows were the kind that never stay on the packages at Christmas. Let me tell you—don't be fooled. Mac's first reaction was to laugh. Then he began to see the novelty in it. He started to try to remove those bows stuck on in those strategic locations—and they wouldn't budge. The next thing you know I'm in extreme pain and using lotions and such to get these damn bows off. It was not the ending I had imagined. Today I have those pink bows prominently displayed in an antique glass. Labeled "Nipples."

❝ People connect with Delta; they feel comfortable around her. They come up to her like she's their sister. And her personal appearances can be very emotional experiences. People line up all around the store just to talk to her, and many who do are crying. Then they put on Delta's designs, and just strut out of the dressing room, saying, 'I've got a shape!' ❞ —Virginia Kearns

Most important, a sense of play can really make a difference in developing your own style. *Fashion should not be work.* Have you ever noticed that the most attractive women seem to bubble over with good cheer? Let a funny hat, a different lipstick, or a new hairstyle give you a lift. If a piece of clothing or a

A sense of play: I entertained the newlyweds Harry and Linda Bloodworth–Thomason as the baton-twirling beauty queen Miss Understood.

Collection of Delta Burke

hairdo makes you feel uneasy or constricted or bogged down, chuck it. Liberate yourself in style. And sometimes you just have to ignore convention and dress to please yourself. My sense of fun and play have landed me on "worst dressed" as well as "best dressed" lists. But it doesn't matter. It made *me* happy and therefore the people around me had fun with it too.

Helping Others Help You

One of the lessons I learned in therapy is that your self-esteem, or lack of it, can have a profound effect on the people around you. A person who is insecure, with a low opinion of herself, may pass blame, become a bully, or infect the entire household with the blues.

On the other hand, the opposite can also be true. While it is in the best interest of everyone around you that you grow and become stronger and more confident, people, being people, sometimes cling to the status quo and stubbornly resist change. Be aware that your partner, friends, and loved ones, being used to the old you, may have their own adjustments to make. And don't let it discourage you if they resist. Remember that when you become stronger and more powerful, you shake up the roles of the people around you. Don't turn away from the people you love; make them feel that they are an integral part of your growth process and an inspiration to you—and they will rise to the occasion.

I'm often asked whether Mac was a help when I was at my lowest. He has always been very supportive of me and very loving. But he also has been overprotective, which a lot of times may not have been in my best interest. It shelters you, inhibits you. Every time I would get a little stronger, it would cause a little shakeup in our relationship. I wouldn't back down around him, which was my old instinct. It was an adjustment for him as well as for me.

Another valuable lesson I learned in therapy was that I cannot change what other people think. The only thing I can control is my reaction. It has been a hard lesson, because sometimes people go too far. I remember on the *Designing Women* set trying to be so good with my diet, eating the right foods all week, keeping my weight down. On film night we'd be on the set until two in the morning, at which time the crew would send out for pizza. Most of the week I would summon up the willpower to ignore the pizza—even if I hadn't eaten all day—but one night I just had to have the damn pizza. I was hungry! So I went to get a slice and suddenly all eyes were on me. People started to make snide remarks.

At that point, the old Delta would generally slink off to her dressing room. I was so beaten down at the time that I couldn't laugh it off. I couldn't simply tell everyone to go jump in a lake and give me another slice, dammit. The new Delta, on the other hand, would have put her therapy into practice. Therapy helped me not to allow my buttons to be pushed, to recognize when I was being pushed too far, and to say no. I've had to learn how not to let things get under my skin. *Let it go*—that's my new mantra.

Your Heart's Desires

What makes *you* happy? What is best for your peace of mind in the long run? We have so many choices in our society now that it's almost impossible to make a clear-cut decision. Sometimes, following your heart's desires is the smartest course to take.

When I was in high school, busy doing all the extracurricular pageants and acting, I felt that nobody really "got" me or understood me. I had one friend in high school whom nobody really "got" either. She was blond and pretty, and—how shall I put it?—*very* stacked. And there I was in my belly-dancing outfits and go-go boots. From our appearances alone, people just naturally assumed we were stuck-up sluts. I'll admit, I was just nuts enough to wear skimpy costumes to school, but I was a hayseed when it came to real sex issues. I had a single-minded ambition and a shameless ignorance about pretty much everything else. It was all a campy spoof—it was show biz! Even when the character of Suzanne was cruel, it wasn't intentional; she was simply blinded by her guileless self-absorption.

The important thing was that none of the talk stopped me from pursuing my goal. For me, dressing up in costumes and being in pageants was simply a means to an end. I was moving away from that world to a world in which I felt I belonged. For my blond friend, however, there was no such outlet. She didn't have those kinds of dreams, and she never left that world. She's been terribly hurt by cruel remarks her whole life and is just now finding her own strength.

The kind of will that is required to chase down your ambitions has to come from within. Remember that old saw about a woman not being whole without a man in her life? Well, to be told that you're not a woman, that you're not sexy, because you don't fit a societal norm—a dress size of 6 or *smaller*—follows the same goofy way of thinking. You know in your heart that both ideas are hogwash. But you have to develop a strong faith in your instincts to battle the powerful messages from society and the media drumming it into your psyche that you are somehow inadequate.

Polite Society

Every actress in Hollywood has a story like this one: An agent jumped me in his office. It was very awkward, because he was working for me at the time. I tried to leave the agency discreetly, but when he got wind of it, he threatened me. I had been trying to avoid a scene and trying to be polite about the whole thing, and all of a sudden *I'm being threatened*. All of a sudden *I'm in danger of losing my livelihood*. Why do I feel I have to apologize for being jumped on?

It's interesting how, when women are sexually harassed, they go out of their way to protect the man's ego. Why do women, particularly women in a vulnerable position, feel they have to concoct an "it's not you, it's me" explanation? Why do we switch the onus to ourselves? We only go home afterward and beat up on ourselves for doing so.

Oh, I did have recourse. I could have gone public. But then I would have been blackballed, careerless, and the object of dirty jokes. I would have suffered the most. If you think this doesn't still go on, you're dead wrong. The actors' union says you have to go public before they'll protect you. I found other well-known actresses had also been attacked—and all of them were too afraid to go public. Unfortunately, the bad guys know this and take advantage of the vulnerable.

It's just another symptom of an impolite society. People don't play by the rules anymore. The simple niceties of life have become outdated. The idea of fair play is becoming a sucker's game. And we as a society lose a little bit of ourselves when we abandon respect and kindness toward each other.

That is the great thing about Mac. He is from the same time and place as I am, someone who understands the rules. He is Southern and he is courtly and he treats everyone with respect.

Without the formal rules of civility, women must instead court power. As such, we can be a force to be reckoned with. Can you imagine what an army of big, beautiful women who believe in fair play and mutual respect could do for this world? Imagine—a column of Amazons bearing this message: We *do* care about manners, we *do* care about kindness, we *do* demand respect. Let's take back our polite society.

You Are a Star

I've always had good posture. Even when I was small, I stood up straight and tall. That's all due to my mother, who said, "Be true to yourself." She instilled in us a deep sense of pride.

When I was in a funk on the set of *Designing Women* and thought everyone hated me and that I looked so awful, I'd practice something that made me feel better. Before taping the show, I had to psych myself up somehow to be able to go out there and perform, make the audience laugh, and for me to forget my own pain or insecurities to withstand whatever might be thrown my way. So before leaving my dressing room, I would face the mirror, stooped in defeat, eyes dead and glazed, skin dull and lifeless. I would stare into my reflection and repeat over and over, *I'm a star, I'm a star, I'm a STAR!* until I began to believe in myself again. In my hypnotic chant, I would see my eyes come to life with fire and sparkle, my skin would glow, and I stood tall and raised my head proudly and suddenly everything clicked. There she was, the one who was strong and resilient and glowing with life. Now I could face anything with grace.

I didn't know it at the time, but I was doing a little self-therapy, reinforcing and reaffirming a belief in myself and my own judgment.

❝ *You can change your behavior through reprogramming the script inside your head—the one that tells you that you are too fat or in some way not worthy, messages you may have learned from childhood on. Break the cycle and the scripted messages by changing the script and then by repeating it over and over, reinforcing it constantly until it is so familiar to you that it becomes second nature. It's not easy. Many of the psychobabble books in stores today make it sound as if change is a snap. To get real change, you need constant reinforcement and support, until not only your thinking and behavior change, but you finally feel the change in your heart. There are many ways to do this: You can try writing exercises or make a tape and listen to it daily. The bottom line is to never lock yourself into a certain way of thinking.* ❞ —Dr. Dennis Cabe

The fact that it worked for me is testament to the power of the mind. You know how getting down on yourself can give you a bad case of the blues? Well, try the opposite: Give yourself a pep talk on a regular basis.

The process continues. It's not like I've got it licked. I have to work on it every day. Sometimes I wake up and feel like a big old cow that nobody wants to see. I have to say, "Delta, you're only going to get older, and you're only going to regret that you didn't live your life fully just because you felt like a dumpling." That alone usually gets me out of bed.

❝ *My favorite story about Delta occurred when she and I were on a USO tour during the Desert Storm offensive in Saudi Arabia. It was a dangerous time. Scud missiles were an everyday danger. We were touring a site when a soldier let us know there were reports of incoming Scud missiles. Delta was signing autographs at the time and just turned to the soldier accompanying us and said, 'You got my gas mask?' and kept right on signing autographs. Cool as a cucumber. I stepped back from her and whistled under my breath. If everyone she'd tussled with in the last few years knew the stuff this gal was really made of, they'd understand the meaning of steel magnolias.* ❞ —Gerald McRaney

Lessons from the Goddesses

All that came with the weight was not negative. It has been for me a journey for inner power, physically and spiritually. I began to stand up for myself. I became much more independent. I learned to let things go. A lot of you are struggling with this— becoming stronger and more empowered while at the same time reinforcing a femaleness that may have been repressed.

I have been doing a lot of reading about the images of the goddesses of ancient lore. I must admit I was somewhat shocked at first by their brazen femininity. The full, voluptuous bodies of the goddesses worshiped by our ancestors are the direct opposite of the body images we're used to seeing. The goddesses were the embodiment of a more powerful woman, one who symbolized fertility, abundance, and strength. Only women could pray to goddesses; men would have to disguise themselves as women to pray. I became particularly enamored of the goddess Nut: the Mother of Rebirth, who beckons in ancient works of art and sculpture with the arms of the great mother. What a comforting thing—a safe, strong, full-bodied woman.

> 66 *The goddess frees women from the limitations of stereotypes. Women can be strong and beautiful.* 99
>
> —Rita M. Gross, *The Book of Goddesses and Heroines*

Today, female images have been sterilized and sanitized. Why, even the process of birth has been taken out of the woman's power into the doctor's hands and hidden away in a sterile hospital room. When I was growing up, everything was painted and sprayed and powdered—reality wasn't dealt with. So much of our power has been taken away from us. And we've let it happen!

It's interesting to look at figures from old times, from Rubens's voluptuous angels to the Victorians in their bustles, when fleshy, full-bodied women were in vogue. In today's society, designers have encouraged women to lose their femaleness in androgynous looks and shapeless bodies. A person having a full, voluptuous, *female* figure these days is perceived as sloppy, undisciplined, lazy, and weak.

One thing I did when I was struggling with all of this was to keep a journal. Writing down what I was going through somehow reinforced and validated my feelings and made the worst of my troubles seem much more bearable. Through exercises that involve writing and drawing your feelings, a workbook allows you to tap into your inner resources and dreams and discard the unimportant things and people that clutter and control your life.

The journal served as a handbook of self-discovery into personal growth, creative expression, and self-healing. As much as I hope *Delta Style* is fun and informative, I also hope it serves as a kind of guide for women to plot their own journeys. A journal can be a key element of that. Think of it as a sit-down talk with yourself, where problems are hashed out and solutions worked on.

You may want to jump-start your journal by answering the following questions. From the answers, you can learn a lot about yourself, the life you lead, and the life you want to lead.

1. What do you most like about yourself? What do other people most like about you?
2. What makes you happy?
3. What clothes lift your spirits?
4. What clothes do you wear the most? What clothes do people tell you look good on you?
5. What is your favorite article of clothing?
6. What is your favorite facial feature? What do people tell you is your best facial feature?
7. When are you most relaxed?
8. How would you change your immediate environment?
9. What is your favorite color? What color do people say you look best in?
10. What is your favorite hair style? What hair style do people say you look best in?
11. You feel powerless when ...
12. You most need ...
13. What kind of work do you do? What kind of work would you like to do?
14. What are your priorities?
15. What scares you?
16. What makes you angry?
17. What makes you sad?

18. What are your talents?
19. When are you at your best?
20. What would you like to improve about yourself?
21. Who is your role model?
22. Who has been your biggest supporter?
23. What was your finest moment so far?
24. What is your most cherished memory?

You can work on problem solving by writing down all of the options, or solutions to the problem, on a piece of paper. Then, in another column, write down and study the ramifications of each option. Most of the time, you already know the answer. Plato said we have the answers inside us. We just have to trust ourselves enough to make the right decisions.

True Grace

One of the biggest misconceptions about real-size people is that they are neither fit, athletic, nor graceful. The truth is that many large people have the same active lifestyles as thin people, and many work out regularly. In fact, for people of all sizes, regular exercise has a tremendously positive effect in boosting self-esteem.

A key element of my turnaround was the self-defense class I took on the set of *Designing Women*. I talked earlier about how the class instructor was a plus size, but because of the way she handled herself, her size became unimportant. She moved with grace and confidence. And I thought, Now that's interesting. Being large doesn't make you a lumbering lug. We can be powerful and strong *and* feminine.

I do a lot of walking now in New Orleans. It gives me a real emotional boost, as well as keeps my heart and lungs strong. If you're reluctant to get out in the world and exercise for fear of being lectured or ridiculed, here are some tips.

- Look for an exercise class that is tailored for the needs of real-size people. Often the local YWCA and community colleges hold classes for plus-size exercisers. Or look for classes that involve low-impact exercises, to protect the joints.
- Wear comfortable shoes with substantial support or use cushion insoles to support the forceful movements.
- Go at your own pace. Don't feel pressured to keep up with others who have been exercising longer.
- Form a walking group. Find a like-minded group of men and women who have time before or after work, and start with a twenty- to thirty-minute stroll three times a week.
- Try yoga classes. Yoga involves stretching, strengthening, and lengthening postures, and each person in class progresses according to his or her own pace. No jumping around or high-impact moves, just relaxing and reenergizing postures built around meditative breathing.

Short-Circuiting Stress

The scariest thing about my stressful time on the *Designing Women* set was the full-blown panic attacks I suffered. They'd have me practically cowering under my bed. I had never had anxiety attacks before, I didn't know what they were, and I had no idea how to deal with them. But I was lucky to have a therapist who helped me work through them. The therapy involved short-circuiting the negative thinking my mind would spiral into when I was feeling overwhelmed or anxious.

Today, with help from the therapy and medication, I bear few residual effects from the panic attacks. Oh, sometimes a paparazzo will jump out of the bushes and give me a start, but I no longer suffer from that kind of debilitating anxiety. Relaxation or breathing exercises help keep me on an even keel and refresh and revitalize me.

If you can give up ten to fifteen minutes a day, you can do

your mind and body a great service. The following easy relaxation exercises can really help reenergize and relax you—and help you cope with the day-to-day stresses.

By the Sea. Lie down on the floor and close your eyes. Imagine that you are at the oceanside, it is a beautiful, warm day, and you are calmly floating in a two-inch pool of water. Visualize the warm sun and the cool water; go up your body in your mind: Feel the water on your toes, on your feet, on your legs, on your back, down your arms, on your hands, on your fingers, back up your arms, on your shoulders, and on your scalp. Repeat for ten to fifteen minutes.

Meditative Breathing. Sit in a dark, quiet room in any comfortable position you choose. Close your eyes and focus on your breathing. Focus on your breath going in and coming out of either your nose or your diaphragm. If your mind wanders, gently return to concentrating on your breath. Do this for at least ten minutes for a remarkably refreshing relaxation.

CHAPTER 3

Let's Play Dress-Up

The Evolution of Delta Style: Clothes as Costume

I was born in high heels. My mother has a home movie of me walking around in her high-heeled shoes on our Florida lawn. I am four years old, garden sprinklers are spraying water everywhere, and little Delta is having no trouble at all maneuvering around in those stiletto heels on that wet lawn. Yes sirree, I took to heels like a duck to water. Years later, as an

actress in Hollywood starring on HBO's *First and Ten,* I played a football team owner who paced the football field in mile-high stilettos. "I don't even know how to *stand* in sneakers," I claimed at the time.

A family photo album holds a snapshot of me at five years old on my way to Gator Land, a theme park featuring alligators. In the photo I am dressed to kill in white gloves, tights, and high heels. I picked out that outfit myself. To visit Gator Land.

From the time I was small I have loved to dress up, occasion or not. For a shy, insecure girl, dramatic costumes provided a thrilling identity to disappear into. The Burkes just took the whole thing a step or two farther. Mother, who had more than a mere flair for the dramatic, loved to create outfits for me: a geisha girl, a gypsy, a pirate, you name it—I was always killing the competition at Halloween costume parties. Even a yard sale became an excuse for the Burkes to dress up; I can still see my grandmother selling old garage tools in a tricornered Revolutionary War hat. (I wore sequins and jewels.)

Mom was a wizard at concocting the most amazing outfits from scraps of material and props she had collected over the years. I remember one outfit in particular, a costume I wore in Orlando's annual Easter Parade when I was sixteen. Nana found a dress that looked as if it had time-traveled straight out of the nineteenth century. It had a frothy little hem and a bustle in pink. Mom finished the look with a saucy little hat and a pink umbrella that I twirled like a parasol. The payoff: the Best-Dressed Individual Costume award for the Orlando Easter Parade of 1972.

But I soon outdid my mother *and* my grandmother. I was the only girl at my first formal dance in junior high draped in a white lace mantilla, for instance, and the only person in the Florida school system to show up in class for Cat Day in black hot pants, fur mittens, a stuffed tail, and little ears.

In my beauty queen days, I went for a different look, despite my natural predilection for flamboyant outfits. I took my job as a representative of the town, state, and fire department very seriously and tried to dress accordingly, in classic, understated styles. The skirts fell way below the knee, the neckline was buttoned up to here, the waistlines were snug but never tight. I wore sensible pumps and neat white gloves and carried an Aunt Bea–style patent-leather pocketbook on one arm. I styled my hair sleek, with a little Dippity-Doo flip on the ends. I'd show up at a Boy Scouts awards ceremony or a nursing home beauty pageant in an understated long-sleeved dress, cinched waist, hide the cleavage. Oh, and the crown. Maybe that's why I dressed conservatively—there aren't many outfits that can compete with a crown.

In full costume for Colonial High's Cat Day. Collection of Delta Burke

When I took the Miss America talent scholarship money and flew to London to study acting, I dragged along my color-coordinated pageant clothes and flipped-up pageant hairpieces. Neither made a big impression at the London Academy of Music and Dramatic Arts. So I grew out of that. I let my hair go wild and witchy and cultivated a more mature look—*very* dramatic, *very* black, Delta *sweeping* through the London fog. My acting school ensemble consisted of a black cane, long black gloves, a black cape, and a black hat with a veil. I carried a silver calling card holder I found at a London flea market, which I flashed while others were reaching for address books. I got out of the airplane wearing that getup

In my personal appearances as a beauty queen, I went the conservative route. Collection of Delta Burke

when I returned home from my two years at the academy. What on earth, my family wondered, is that?

In Hollywood I auditioned for and won a part as a leather-bound dominatrix in *Temporary Insanity* and entered what I refer to as my Betty Page phase. Betty Page was a famous 1950s calendar pin-up girl who wore lots of sexy black leather and heels. To get a feel for the character, I visited the grocery store

I went to London a model of decorum, in tasteful, coordinated outfits.

Collection of Delta Burke

and the bank in a leather skirt, red corset, black cross-strapped heels, and black fishnet hose. Reactions were mixed: People were either real friendly or somewhat appalled. After we finished filming, I felt naked unless I was body-wrapped in leather. Producers would ask my agent why I was dressed like that. I'd go to auditions in that outfit and then run home to my grandmother and play Scrabble. Nana, having a highly developed sense of drama herself, barely blinked.

I recognized early on that contemporary clothes didn't work any particular magic on me. Put me in clothes from other eras, however, and I become something special. I could pull off that va-va-va-voom look—it was *me*, it was my figure. I guess I was born in the wrong era.

When I found peplum, now, *that* was Suzanne Sugarbaker! You can look back at the shows and watch how, as the character of Suzanne became clearer, the clothes evolved with her. As Suzanne became more comfortable with her body, she became more confident in her dress: She took on bright hues and cinched waists and short skirts—and everything became bigger and brassier and sassier. She developed a strong, distinctive style.

By the time my next show, *Delta,* started shooting, I went to extremes to get away from the character of Suzanne. I dyed my hair blond and went from peplum to country music–style 1950s outfits. Four years later, when I was asked to come back and reprise the role of Suzanne, on the sitcom *Women of the House,* I first found the transition awkward. I—Delta—had moved on in so many ways. But Suzanne had developed into a full-bodied character physically and emotionally in the later years on *Designing Women,* so that falling back into her patterns soon became as easy as falling off a chair.

In the past few years I've been able to satisfy my costume addiction on a regular basis during Mardi Gras in New Orleans. My outfits are outrageously colorful and glittery—one was even designed by Hollywood's famed designer Bob

I like clothes with a period feel. This one, on the set of James Brolin's Hotel, has a nice 1940s feeling to it. Collection of Delta Burke

Mackie—but they're tame in comparison to those worn by other revelers at Mardi Gras time.

All my life, wearing costumes and taking on glamorous personas have allowed me to escape from reality—it's a continuation of playing dress-up in my attic room and disappearing into fantasies. I still love costumes, but the big difference is, *now the clothes I wear reflect what's going on inside me.*

Playing dress-up is also a thread of memory, linking me forever to my mother and grandmother and reminding me of happy times. And I have carried on the tradition. In 1995, my dog Bitsy was named the Grand Marshall of Barkus, the Mardi Gras parade for dogs. Bitsy is a little mutt I adopted on a movie set, where her asthma was so bad that Bitsy's owner had thoughts of putting her down. I took her home, and four years later Bitsy is happy and healthy. So healthy, in fact, that I had no trepidations having Mom sew some plastic bones to a large sock that we poked holes in for Bitsy's legs and head. Mom even fixed it so the bones looked like they were hanging from her ears. I accompanied Bitsy with a bone through my head and a bone scepter in my hand. Bitsy, being a true ham in the best Burke tradition, loved every minute of it.

Dressing the Real-Size Woman

From all the images that come at us in advertisements, in magazines, and on television, you'd think that the average American woman's dress size was a 4 or 6. The reality: The average American woman is a size 12, what fashion designers call a *hard* 12, which is actually somewhere between 12 and 14.

The reason most people don't know that there are sixty-five million American women who are size 12 and up is that for too long these women have been snubbed by designers and clothing manufacturers alike. I discovered this when I went looking for clothes that fit me. I'd see cute clothes in a magazine but couldn't find the same, up-to-date styles in my own size. It appeared that once you hit a certain weight, you lose interest in style and relinquish your sexuality, your personality, even your brains.

But all that is changing rapidly. Real-size women represent not only the size 22s, but the size-12 and -14 baby boomers and working mothers who aren't interested in giving up eating but find themselves abandoned by clothing manufacturers. Excuse me, but women who have had babies do *not* have the flat stomachs of teenagers. Oh, sure, you can get a washboard belly if you have lots of money to spend on exercising six hours a day or having the fat suctioned off. But how far will we go in mutilating ourselves simply to fit someone else's notion of beauty?

I'm not the only one having trouble finding things to wear. Here's a letter I got from a twenty-three-year-old real-size woman in Boston:

> I am not at all ashamed of my appearance, and believe I am a beautiful person, inside and out. Can you help get the word out to designers? First, we don't want to dress like old ladies. Second, not every heavy woman is 10 feet tall. Third, we want clothes that make us feel beautiful, look beautiful, and act beautiful!

And this, from Texas:

> I am an attorney practicing with a prestigious firm in the competitive Texas legal market. As you can imagine, I am expected to dress conservatively, but with an eye to current styles and some flair. While the price of clothing is not a big issue for me, the lack of professional business attire available in my size is a real dilemma. Even stylish casual clothing is hard to find. This is complicated by the fact that at 5' 2" tall, I simply cannot carry many of the plus-size fashions in stores today.

One more, from Sacramento:

> I find very little selection in sexy lingerie, short jacket suits that emphasize waists, or sundresses. I would also like to see more consideration for moderately priced clothes that do not contain polyester.

It's no wonder so many have felt so insecure about shopping for clothes. It made me determined to see that all women have the opportunity to dress with flair and be comfortable in their clothes.

I have also come to grips with the fact that I will never be a size 6 again. I'll likely be big and curvy, no matter what. So I decided that I could be big, bright, and happy—or I could be big, drab, and unhappy. I mean, look at me. I've got this body. I've got these boobs. I've got these hips. Put a tent on me, and I'm going to look like a tent. So, okay, I look like a big, curvy woman. But I look like a *woman*.

What Do Real-Size Women Want?

❝ Delta knows the plus-size woman's body better than anyone. She is that woman. And she lives her life according to how she feels, not how someone tells her she should feel. Whatever weight she's at, she makes it work for her. ❞

—Barry Zelman, designer

The letters I've gotten from all over the country have been helpful to me not only in a supportive sense. Your comments are the driving force behind my clothing line. When I asked my Advisory Council to describe a wish list for clothing, the same phrases kept popping up. More choices. Quality, construction-fit clothing. Sexy style. People designing real-size clothes who are real-size women. Here are a few specific things real-size ladies would like to see more of:

- Soft, natural fabrics that flow
- Comfortable but not frumpy clothes
- No more smocks or sacks
- Sweatshirts without cute animals or giant flowers on them
- Young styles
- Bright, vibrant colors
- No cheesy fabrics with little old lady styles
- Sexy lingerie—we want to look pretty, too!
- Good-fitting jeans that don't ride up
- Well-proportioned armholes and legs, which are often too big in large sizes
- Elastic waists that don't ride up
- Longer shirttails that stay tucked in
- More feminine looks—but no more ruffles!
- Pantsuits that fit top and bottom
- Better-fitting bras
- Wardrobe that lasts—no shoddy seamwork or hems

It's obvious that we know our bodies well. And we know that we deserve and require special attention. There is nothing more precision-oriented than designing for real women. It's a real science. The armholes must be relaxed enough for a woman to have comfort and movement. A top must have vents and lengths that won't pull at the rear. The chest area of a top must have darts on certain styles that flatter, not flatten, a woman's bust. The bottoms must be generous in the inseam and outseam so that the woman feels comfortable without feeling constricted. The clothes in general have to be well pro- portioned.

We have all been in outfits that take over the body. You

walk into a room and the clothes take on a separate identity. You feel disembodied. Don't let an outfit wear you; you should wear the outfit. Your clothes should harmonize with your body and express how you're feeling from the inside out. Clothes should also follow your natural shape. You're only as wide as your widest line. So, for example, you may be calling attention to the widest part of you when you wear jackets that stop at the widest part of your hips or wear skirts that end at the widest point on your legs.

Dressing your form is more than just science and sizing. There is a magic that occurs when we wear something that not only fits us well but makes us feel good and confident in the bargain.

The Components of Delta Style

All of us have unique fashion preferences. I love fitted things, fitted bodices, peplum or safari jackets. I wear bright colors simply because I like them and I like the way I feel in them, but I also love the drama of black. Clothes that are sexy and sassy make me feel empowered. The bottom line is individual taste. I say provide options, and let the individual make up her own mind. Below are my choices for a well-balanced wardrobe.

❝ *Delta style is feminine and strong; it's about breaking rules. It's about anything that has a great-looking fabric or brightly colored print; it's about not shying away from cleavage or short skirts. It's about big, romantic hats and costume jewelry and cinchy belts and pretty buttons.* ❞ —Barry Zelman

Color Your World

1
2
2

My sense of color is a bit, shall we say, overstated. I have a thing for pink. When Nana and I lived in Los Angeles and spent our days nosing around in flea markets and yard sales, we brought home a lot of what others might call junk. Whatever it was, it would have to compete with the Pepto-Bismol hot-pink walls of our apartment. When Mac and I first lived together, my motto was, paint it pink and stick it in the living room. Whether it was an art deco footstool or a store mannequin we proclaimed "artistic," we painted it pink and stuck it in the living room.

I still like pink. My New Orleans living room has fabrics in pink and red. I recently read that pink is one of the most soothing colors for walls. It certainly has a calming effect on me, like being in the womb.

It's said that people are influenced by color more than any other design aspect. That may be because color can influence mood, personality, and attitude. Fashion is color driven as well. It's a fashion industry truism that if you have a garment that has great style and the color doesn't work, the piece won't sell. Don't overdo color: Use it as you would anything else, with a deft touch. A real-size lady can easily brighten up her face with a jewel-toned scarf or an electric-blue hat. Or dress up a simple black dress with a richly colored shawl or a sparkly sweater.

Fabricatin'

In the fourth season of *Designing Women,* when I was feeling really big, Cliff Chally, the show's designer, and I worked together to create outfits from gauzy, floating fabrics. Light fabrics, I knew, soften the shape and don't add thickness to the body. The clothes Cliff created were dramatic yet feminine. I felt as if I were floating when I made an entrance. They made me feel prettier.

Soft, flowing fabrics, clothes that sweep with liquid fabrication, have a sensual quality. I love the feel of silk, 100-percent cotton knit, cashmere, soft rayon blends, even pliable prewashed denim. Perhaps all those years of being force-fed unappealing fabrics made us real-sizers appreciate lush fabrics even more.

Knowing about fabric can tell you a lot about how a

1
2
3

garment will work out. Second-rate fabrics simply don't last or wear as well as quality fabrics. When buying clothes, look at the label. Note the percentage of natural fibers, such as cotton, silk, or wool, to artificial, such as polyester, Lycra, nylon, spandex. Often the synthetics have been added to make the gar-

I love costumes. Here I played a circus performer in The Fall Guy.

Collection of Delta Burke

ment easier to care for or to help it hold its shape. New technology has improved the quality of many synthetics, but on the whole, the longer-lasting and better-quality fabrics contain a higher percentage of natural fibers. A lot depends on your needs: Do you want something that doesn't require dry cleaning or hand washing? Then you should look for blends. Do you prefer breathable fabrics? Look for cottons, silks, or rayon or viscose blends. Do you want a fabric that can double for work and evening wear? Go for silk. Also, look at and feel the garment. Does it have nubs that get caught on your skin? Does it drape nicely? Does it have elasticity when you gently tug on it? The bottom line: Wear fabrics you are most comfortable in.

Construction Fit

One of the most stirring times I've had in my life was the USO goodwill trip Mac and I took to Saudi Arabia during the Desert Storm operation. I was thrilled to be meeting General Norman Schwarzkopf and talking with our troops in Saudi Arabia, but I most emphatically did *not* look forward to wearing those USO battle fatigues. They did not have construction-fit seaming; they simply *hung* there. So I had a set of fatigues altered just for me, construction-fit, with darts. They even had cute little shoulder pads. Unfortunately, I was allowed only one piece of luggage on the trip, and that piece was lost somewhere over the Atlantic Ocean. Scud missiles, be damned, I felt like shouting, find those fatigues! No dice. Oh, well, I thought, getting into some loose-hanging, unpadded battle fatigues, when all else fails, go with personality.

Many plus-size clothing lines are merely extensions of a designer's misses line and do not have the construction fit that real sizes need. A real-size woman needs clothes that work with her body. Look for clothing with princess seams, which fit the body's contours. These take more time to make but fit the body better and show the figure better.

1
2
5

Clothesless at Desert Storm: Not only were my specially made fatigues lost, but I got blisters from wearing Army combat boots. Here I'm being Band-Aided with the help of General Schwarzkopf and my husband.

Collection of Delta Burke

Sexy Dressing

A woman's neckline is one of the most beautiful of God's creations. So why do so many designers feel the need to cover up real-size necks? I like to show off my neck with V necks—they elongate the neck. You can do the same with jewel necks, scoop necklines, crew necks. On the other hand, I like turtleneck dressing—but then I wear a jacket with a plunging neckline over the turtleneck, which still emphasizes the length of the neck.

I like to play up my curves with peplum jackets and fitted waistlines. I also like to wear what I call "glamour blouses," oversize button-down shirts with plunging necklines, great prints, and sexy, silky fabrication, over a slim pair of pants.

Accessorize!

The Crown Jewels. A common mistake that real-size women make is piling on the jewelry! I guess it's an attempt to cover up or camouflage. Don't detract from your inner beauty. One great piece can do more for an outfit than tons piled on—a great pair of gold earrings, for example, or a jewel-tone scarf, a slim belt, a wide-brimmed hat.

Fancy Feet. Okay, my personal preference: stilettos with at least four-inch heels. Anything, as Mac likes to say, to really cripple the feet. Otherwise, I wear boots: hiking boots, boots with heels, black lace-up boots, boots with pointy toes, all kinds of boots.

For all of you sensible gals, you should never wear shoes that are too small. You will end up with corns and calluses that can be difficult to get rid of, and your feet will *look* uncomfortable as well, all wedged up in too small a space.

Look for shoes that flatter. Opt for curved or tapered toe boxes. A square toe box will make big feet look twice as big. If you have trouble finding shoes that fit, you may want to look into custom-made shoes. Also, many catalogs specialize in shoes that are constructed in wide widths. I've also found that there are certain looks and styles that work well for me and I tend to favor them, whether they are in fashion or not. You don't have to be a slave to fashion. Stick to what works best for you and makes you feel the most comfortable. A good example is how I dressed as a contestant at Miss Florida. My clothes weren't fashionable but they were classics and could therefore stand the test of time better than the fashions of the 1970s that my peers were wearing. But mainly I dressed that way because it's how I felt comfortable and how I felt a Miss Florida should look.

Lingerie. I don't like lingerie that reveals your charms before you're ready to show them. My favorite lingerie look, a gown with matching robe, lets you make your entrance with all things covered. It also lets you exit a room without having to back out. You can reveal your charms at your discretion.

Leg Work. I'm not wild about panty hose. I like the kind that give you support but not the kind you have to fight all the way up. Don't you hate having to battle your panty hose every step of the way, from your foot to your thigh? I think that if men had to wear them, panty hose would be outlawed.

But in my work I'm forced to deal with panty hose, as most real-size working women do. On the plus side, panty hose can be a fun, inexpensive way to dress up your wardrobe or give it some flash. Try textured, or fishnet, hosiery with the right outfit. Black or dark-colored hosiery does wonders: It make legs appear slimmer and goes with just about anything.

Capes. I am sure there is some seminal connection to my attraction for capes from the pageant days, when draping myself in those plush velvet-and-ermine capes gave me an electric rush. I still love capes: You've got your high drama, your flair, and your practical use from the warmth. Capes are perfect for real-size ladies—they're not only stylish and unique but they're comfortable, roomy, and nonconstricting as well. Capes, like lingerie sets, also allow you to reveal or conceal your charms when *you* decide.

Bathing Beauties. As a guest star on three *Love Boat* episodes, I knew that every *Love Boat* has a scene where everyone is parked around the swimming pool. At the time of my first appearance, I was a size 6 or 8, but I was still convinced my hips and thighs were not fit for television. So when the dreaded swimming pool scene came up, I was ready for it. I came up with a sexy sarong to hide my hips and legs. It gave it some oomph and I got myself off the hook, as well. That sarong is now in my clothing line.

Real-size ladies are in luck these days with all the choices in swimwear. Many one-piece suits now have amazing panels containing midriff-controlling or side-shirring fabrics, such as Lycra. If you have a pear shape, choose suits that draw the eye up and enhance your shoulders and bust. If you are round in the middle, de-emphasize your waist and choose suits with princess seams. Many manufacturers sell tops and bottoms in separate sizes, so you can get the right fit in both. Or get creative: Wrap a sarong around your suit; buy a suit with a skirt; play up your beautiful cleavage.

Dueling Outfits

Mac also likes costumes. He just doesn't seem to know that he likes costumes. He doesn't even seem to realize that he *wears* costumes. All the time. He thinks it's normal to get dressed to go to the grocery store in an English gentleman's hunting outfit. He likes to hit the post office in a safari ensemble. When he was working on *Major Dad,* I thought the marines had landed.

Doing errands around town, he'll pull on a T-shirt and some britches that he most likely slept in. But when we get ready to go to our farm in Mississippi, that's when Mac likes to get *really* done up. On go the tweeds, the vest, the tie, the knee-high lace-up snakeproof boots he designed himself. It's Mac in his gentleman planter's mode—and he looks good, I must admit. He's got the whole look down. "But we are going to plant potatoes," I say. Which leads to a conversation that goes something like this:

MAC: *Delta, I wear my boots because the farm is full of snakes in winter.*
DELTA: *Well, honey, that makes you the best-looking man in the swamp.*
MAC: *(pause) I think that's what's known as a backhanded compliment.*

I guess I just don't have the flair for farm dressing that Mr. Gerald McRaney does.

Unfortunately, Mac and I have a slight problem coordinating our wardrobes. One instance in particular stands out—when Mac and I were invited to Elizabeth Taylor's gala sixtieth birthday party. It was my first outing as a blonde, and I wanted to look especially good for the celebration. I chose a hot-pink suede jacket to go with my new blond hair.

Because I was out getting my roots done, I didn't get to see

A typical Mac outfit to go shopping in. As is required of all male members of any tribe, he is a-totin' his wife's "extry" bag. Collection of Delta Burke

Mac before the party. So I show up in head-to-toe pink, and there's Mac, with a big grin on his face, happy to see me—in a *bright red blazer*. I think I gasped or something, because Mac immediately came over to see if I was all right. "We're gonna clash!" I said with clenched teeth.

This is a concept that Mac does not understand—that when we walk side by side or he hugs me close, we very well may be blinding innocent people. I know with our schedules it's hard to plan, but we *never* look like we should be together. I'll come out of my dressing room wearing some conservative suit with con-servative pumps, and he'll be standing there in lederhosen.

In spite of my mortification, no one at Elizabeth Taylor's birthday party seemed to notice—consider the competition— and Mac and I had a great time. I went home with a wad of napkins to shellac, which is sort of a hobby for me. I hung up my pretty pink outfit, and Mac put his blazing red blazer away. No, sir, it wasn't the first time—and it wouldn't be the last— that Mac and I have shown up in dueling outfits.

A Few Easy Pieces

I firmly believe you should build on what you have in your closet, not buy something to wear once or twice. My favorite pieces to build on include a casual tunic with slits; leggings; a long blazer; a short, tight skirt; a long, flowing skirt; and an old-fashioned dress with a colorful print and a tiered effect, layered at the bottom—short in front to show off my legs and long in back. Here are a few ways to mix and match.

For day to day, I have my "uniform," my comfortable casual clothes. This consists of a shirt or blouse with an open jewel neck or V neck, a shirt or jacket (fitted waist), black leggings, and black boots. I top it all off with a black flamenco-style hat.

The Top Ten Fashion Myths

Every woman who has shopped for plus-size clothing recognizes the same dull merchandise. Someone, somewhere, decreed that certain fashion styles were off-limits to real-size women. Once and for all, we would like to put to rest those old chestnuts.

Myth #1. You Must Wear Monochromatic Colors. What colors you wear should depend entirely on the colors you *like* and which hues best match your hair, eyes, and skin color. For example, I wear a lot of blue, as the color intensifies my blue eyes. My favorite is periwinkle blue, but I also love bright jewel tones and flowery prints. Don't be afraid of color!

Myth #2. Horizontal Stripes Are Out. It all depends on the way a piece is designed. If an outfit has the proper cut and design, horizontal stripes can be quite flattering.

Myth #3. Don't Wear Clinging Fabrics. Why not look and feel sexy? I can't get enough of a soft, beautifully draped fabric, like silk, challis, crepe, rayon, or cotton knitwear. Many of the new fabrics, including tencel, are sumptuous feeling and looking. These fabrics don't pull or stick but follow the curves of the body nicely, giving you the luxurious feel of flowing liquid fabrication.

First you have to get them to notice you before they pull in and buy! Nana and me in costume for a yard sale.
Collection of Delta Burke

Steel magnolias. My entourage from the pageant days included (from left) chaperone Jean Miller, Mom, Nana, and chaperones Dotty Cagna and Marilyn Masters. Collection of Delta Burke

Pageant regulars called me "Snow White."
Ed Stout

Note my conservative dress compared with that of the other Miss America contestants, all decked out in 1970s bell-bottoms.

Hess Photography, Atlantic City

Maybe I've overaccessorized for a swim. I was celebrating my twenty-sixth birthday at a pool party.
Collection of Delta Burke

Clever poolside attire: I solved the problem of hiding my hips in <u>Love</u> <u>Boat</u> bathing-suit scenes with this sarong.
Collection of Delta Burke

I wore my vintage leopard coat to the <u>Mike Hammer</u> set.
Collection of Delta Burke

I loved wearing my mother's 1950s clothes in A Bunny's Tale.
Collection of Delta Burke

The camera getting a shot of my stilettos doing that sexy dominatrix walk in a TV movie, <u>Temporary Insanity</u>, where I played a character named Big Woman. I loved this kind of over-the-top look. Collection of Delta Burke

One of my va-va-va-voom outfits, in <u>The</u> <u>Lottery</u>.
Collection of Delta Burke

Pink redux: Me with Mama Jean, playing a <u>Designing Women</u> guest, at the wedding of Jean Smart's character, Charlene.

Gene Arias

A country-western look for Delta.

Photofest (*Delta*). Bob D'Amico

A couple of swellegant dressers.
Collection of Delta Burke

Some say I have a penchant for blue. But there's <u>blue</u> (here with Betty White and Blanche backstage at <u>The Hollywood Squares</u>) . . .

Collection of Delta Burke

. . .jazzed up blue (here with James Brolin on the set of Hotel) . . .
Collection of Delta Burke

. . . and then there's <u>serious</u> blue (here with Mama at my engagement party).
Collection of Delta Burke

Myth #4. Pass up Short Skirts. Never! Short skirts free the body to move and show off great-looking legs. Not too short, however: One or two inches above the knee is a flattering, comfortable length.

Myth #5. Layering Adds Bulk. Not if the fit is good. Put peplum jackets over bias-cut skirts; long, construction-fit blazers over short skirts; narrow silky tunics over leggings.

Myth #6. Forget Plunging Necklines. Show off that cleavage, girl! My line of clothing features all sorts of neckline options: scoop necks, round necks, crew necks. A V-neck style actually makes your neck look thinner and longer.

Myth #7. Pleats Are Unflattering. It's all about construction fit, working with a woman's pattern and silhouette, and not trying to make her fit into something that's not made with her body shape in mind. The key to great pleats is draping, not pulling. You need only ensure that the pleats have the proper closure. When you close it up, it should fall into place nicely.

Myth #8. Don't Do Denim. This is a great casual look for big women, and too many shy away from it because they feel jeans are too confining. But with the soft-style and easy-style denims on the market, jeans can be terrific. Ours are made with a contoured waist, proportioned to fit. As the sizes go up, so does the scale of the pockets and belt loops. Contoured yokes are designed to fit the woman's waistline. I for one don't like that whole elastic business. There are other things you can do to make jeans and pants fit around the waist and still curve at the hips without resorting to elastic waists. However, in my line I offer both options because some women still feel most comfortable with elastic.

Myth #9. Waistbands Are for Skinnies. A cinched waist is one of the most attractive styles going, particularly on zaftig hourglass figures. It's all about proportion and balance.

Myth #10. The Only Fashion Choice: Caftans. Again, a limited mind-set in a changing world and one probably perpetuated by tent makers. Large-size women have the same fashion needs as everyone else: They need career wear, sportswear, evening wear, and sleepwear.

Delta's Ten Commandments of Clothing Style

1. Allow color to set the tone for your outfit.

2. Wear clothes that make you feel comfortable and secure.

3. Clothing that has the right fit and construction will always flatter the shapes of a woman's body.

4. Don't be afraid of prints and patterns that reflect your personality.

5. Wear accessories that enhance an outfit, not overpower it.

6. Clothes are what you wear, not who you are.

7. Confidence, style, and attitude come from within and should be expressed with what you wear and how you feel when you wear it.

8. Don't be afraid to take chances with your wardrobe when it comes to overcoming the taboos of fashion.

9. Think about the parts of your body that you like and buy clothes that accentuate those areas with style and sophistication.

10. Stop thinking that you can't. You *can* wear clothes that are a reflection of who you are and allow you to evolve into who you want to be.

Best Fits for Your Shape

Like the fashion myths, fashion dictates should be taken with a grain of salt. But with all the new choices opening up for real-size women, some professional fashion advice may be welcome. What follow, then, are some gentle *suggestions* on the types of clothes that are most flattering to each body type. Again, style is subjective and entirely personal. Use these suggestions as a starting point.

Boxy Shape
- Create curves with elastic waistlines.
- Try drop-waisted looks such as blouson shirts or poet's shirts.
- Emphasize the shoulders with shoulder pads.
- Wear long tunics, with side vents or slits or buttons.
- Wear a shell or layering piece underneath jackets or tunics.
- Wear straight, long tunics or, for shape, implied shapings (beautifully cut shirts, blouses, for example).
- Show off good legs with short skirts and tunics.
- Wear soft fabrics.
- Dress in layers.

Pear Shape, Heavy Hips or Thighs
- Wear flowing, easy fabrics on bottom.
- Balance top and bottom. Highlight shoulder area. Wear shoulder pads; give the illusion of shape and waist.

- Don't wear tight leggings with tighter top.
- Wear wide collars.
- Drape a colorful sweater around your shoulders.
- Wear soft overblouses that don't cling.

Large, Round Middle
- Create a waist with elastic waistbands or take the emphasis away from the torso by highlighting the hips and shoulders.
- Wear full top, tighter bottom.
- Wear leggings or short skirts with oversize tunics with shoulder pads.
- Wear shirts that narrow at the hem.

Quick Fixes

Small Waist
- Emphasize waist, but not so severely that top and bottom appear out of proportion. Wear peplum or cinched belts.
- V necks are flattering.
- Wear blouses that taper at the waist and flair out slightly.

Narrow Shoulders
- Wear shoulder pads.
- Wear boat necks.
- Avoid tight tops.

Small Bustline
- Wear jewel necklines.
- Wear shirts with ruffles, gathers, or tucks.
- Wear roomy tops like cable-knit sweaters.
- Empire waistlines are flattering.

Large Bustline
- Wear revealing necklines—don't hide it. But show cleavage diplomatically, of course.
- Be very careful with shoulder pads—too big and you end up looking like a football player.
- Make sure your garment is fitted with darts with plenty of armhole and neckhole room so that it doesn't pull in the chest.
- Consider a minimizer bra to control and shape.
- Wear light, fluid fabrics like silks and rayons.

Plus-Size Arms

- Wear relaxed armholes that don't have that embarassing "pulling." Best sleeve length: right at the elbow.

Heavyset Legs

- Don't put skirt length in the middle of the calf. Keep skirts and lines flowing, long or short.
- If you wear straight skirts, you'll need fuller shirts and shoulder pads.
- Wear shoes that elongate the leg, such as styles with a low-cut vamp, like mules. Few people can get away with wearing chunky heels without their legs looking bigger; wear heels that have a slender, graceful curve instead. But not too high: Stiletto-type shoes will make your proportions look off.

Big Rear End

- Make sure the silhouette is right for the figure. Long plus-size cut is generous, working in a straight line rather than an A-line, which will cause "pulling." No peplum: The eye goes straight to the butt.
- Wear a printed or color tunic as the focal piece of outfit. Work with it, not against it. Use an eye-catching top with a solid bottom.
- Wear prints and color on top; low-key, mono-chromatic color on bottom. Example: black ciga-rette pants with a splashy print shirt on top.

Tall and Real Size

- Find well-fitting clothes in the men's department. Look for long, full shirts and sweaters and tall lengths in jackets.

Petite and Real Size

- Don't clutter up your look; keep the details, treatments, and accessories light.
- Wear soft, light fabrics.

Traveling Light

I used to travel in Hollywood high fashion—me and about fifty pieces of luggage. Since I left the West Coast, everything about my life has been whittled down and simplified. The entourage is gone. You too can get rid of the clutter you drag around with you by making clothes work double duty. Plan your wardrobe around a few classic pieces and use accessories and detailing to jazz them up.

Here's what I wear to travel:

1. Leggings, which I live in. You can build your entire wardrobe around leggings.
2. Hiking boots, for shopping, walking, exercising.
3. Button-down shirt over my leggings.
4. Traveling vest, which is a photographer's vest that I got in a sporting goods catalog. It's great—it's got tons of pockets so that all my important things are right there at my fingertips.
5. Hat—always.

In the suitcase I carry:

1. A pretty blouse to go over my leggings.
2. A nice pair of boots and a pair of heels—to dress up my leggings for evening.
3. T-shirt.
4. Throw a belt in there, for a different look with a different shirt.
5. Basic jewelry. I like gold earrings and a gold chain with a locket or trinket on the end. I can get different looks, from upscale to downscale, by changing what's on the end of that chain.

CHAPTER 4

Let's Face It: Skin Care and Makeup

Makeup and the Real-Size Woman

People sometimes ask me at what point in my makeup routine do I become Delta Burke—you know, that big-haired lady with the Kabuki makeup? I can track the different Deltas by the layers of makeup I'm wearing:

Delta #1: No makeup.

Delta #2: One level up: a painted mouth, sunglasses on, hair up in hat. I wear this coming in to the L.A. airport, 'cause I know the paparazzi are always there.

Delta #3: Add mascara. Add more mascara.

Delta #4: Add eyeliner. There she is: Delta Burke.

I'm a big believer in eyeliner. But I overdosed on that heavy-duty made-up look when I was living in Los Angeles and working long weekly hours on the set of *Designing Women*. Every weekend became *maintenance weekend*. Manicure, pedicure, facial—you name it. It became a chore. I never had any time for myself. I'd either be "on" or sleeping or in a maintenance mode.

Then when I turned thirty-six, I started going a little nuts. I felt I had to get those big lips like the models have, to keep myself looking young and in the ingenue business. So I had collagen injections in my lips. It was too subtle looking to make a difference, but it had other effects that were not so subtle. I could not move my face. That collagen was so stiff I could barely smile or make funny faces. And my making the faces is what my comedy is all about. So big lips was a big washout. Also, it hurt like hell!

My attempts to recapture my youth took on much less importance when I moved to New Orleans. My whole glam routine loosened up. I didn't get a facial for two years. My life was about unpacking boxes and fixing up the house and digging potatoes at the farm. I even have a farmer's tan, which would have been sacrilege in Los Angeles; if you put my hands against my legs, they look like they belong to another human being.

Even more amazing to everyone who knows me is the fact that I can walk out of my house without a stitch of makeup and not flinch. This is the same girl my mother sent to London where the other academy students took bets on whether I could go a day without makeup. In two years, I never did.

The no-makeup Delta on a camping trip in the early 1980s. (But I did take along my tiara and scepter!) Collection of Delta Burke

Don't Overdo It

One thing we real-size ladies should never do is exaggerate or overdo our makeup. I know this firsthand: I've done a lot of experimenting on myself over the years. When I lived in London and couldn't sleep, I would practice making up my

1
4
5

The many faces of Delta: makeup Polaroids on the set over the years. From top: Charleston, 1978, Temporary Insanity, 1985, Redbook, 1989.

Collection of Delta Burke

From top: Designing Women, *1986,* Day-O, *1991,* Where the Hell's That Gold, *1988.* Collection of Delta Burke

face all night. The later it got, the goofier I looked. I usually ended up falling asleep in full clown face.

I took this shot of myself in goofy makeup late at night in London. It still makes me laugh. Collection of Delta Burke

But after working with the best makeup artists in the world, I've learned ways to enhance my face without looking like Bette Davis playing Baby Jane. Concentrate instead on your best facial feature and accent that. I like to give my blue eyes a lot of play. This also takes the emphasis off what you might consider to be lesser assets. But you can do something about those too. For example, my upper lip is kind of thin, so I have learned how to extend the line of the lip—but just slightly. Many actresses of the 1930s and 1940s, like Joan Crawford and Lucille Ball, went a little overboard—just look at those lips! If you're making up your face for daytime, go easy on the lips. Otherwise you'll have people coming up to you and saying, "What the heck is that on your lip?" When I'm working in front of a camera, I need that exaggerated line, but if I wear too much in everyday use, I look at myself in the mirror and wonder, Whose mouth is this?

Some real-size ladies also overdo it when it comes to contouring. According to my makeup artist friends, everybody needs some kind of corrective contouring, which emphasizes the angles and planes of the face. Blending is the key to avoiding obvious contouring, which usually appears as one big brown smear right next to skin that is an entirely different color. Find a contour powder that is slightly darker than your skin, and blend it into the jawline, under the chin, and directly under the cheek line in an upward motion. Use a small cosmetic sponge to smudge and blend all contour lines.

Watch out for that apple-cheek look as well. Putting a round dab of blush on your cheeks can make your face look rounder. Apply blush directly under your cheek line and upward toward your temples to give your cheekbones definition.

It's fun to do a real glamour job on your face every now and then, but that whole business of women covering up, concealing, and hiding under layers of war paint simply to face the world is a bunch of baloney. I've become quite comfortable greeting the world in my own face, thank you. I say real beauty will out.

❝ *True beauty comes from within; everything else is artificial and will be detected as such. Some of the most interesting and attractive women I have ever known were not perfect beauties by any means, but their energy and self-assurance gave them admirers by the score.* ❞

—Dr. Forrest C. Brown, dermatologist and dermatological surgeon

Skin Care and the Real-Size Woman

❝*As a makeup artist, I'm always anxious to see the actor's skin before the project to discern how much 'repair work' will be involved. On a very cold winter's day at six o'clock in the morning, I was waiting to meet Delta Burke. She stepped into the makeup trailor, not a stitch of makeup on; her dark, thick hair was everywhere. She was wearing a goose-down jacket, black leggings, black leather boots, and a black leather tote bag with a two-pound Yorkie stuffed inside it, its little head popping out. She smiled and said, 'Hi, I'm Delta, and this is Loretta.' I was sort of dumbfounded and blurted out, 'Oh, my heavens, you look like a child. Your skin is flawless.' Then I asked her to take out her color contacts. She said she wasn't wearing any. Her eyes are as blue as the ocean. My job had just become easier.***❞*

—Cassandra Scott

Have you ever noticed that many real-size women have lovely skin? It's been reported that a little extra padding may actually prevent wrinkles and gives skin a youthful appearance. Even so, you should never neglect the care of your skin. Skin is like a canvas; if you have a damaged canvas, it's difficult to paint a picture on it. Your number-one priority in skin care is keeping the canvas clean and blemish free. Real-size women may be tempted to buy tightening products to offset fleshiness in the face. But you should avoid anything that pulls your skin taut. Skin is like a rubber band: The more you pull and contract it, the less elastic it becomes.

Good grooming makes a big impression out in the world. But choosing which products to use can be confusing, considering the quantities of skin care brands on the market. What you should look at even more than the ingredients is the grade, or density, of those ingredients. An inexpensive grade of mineral oil is bad for the skin. A fine grade of mineral oil is good for the skin. The same theory applies to alcohol. You've probably heard not to put alcohol on your skin, right? But alcohol can be beneficial if the grade is fine. Dyes and preservatives are always presumed to be bad for the skin, but this too depends on the grade of the dye. Consult a beauty salon aesthetician or dermatologist to find the right combination for you.

Sun Baby

I was not only the youngest Miss Florida, I was one of the first Miss Floridas without a tan. Growing up in the Sunshine State with pale white skin was like being a poodle in a kennel full of rottweilers. How I wanted a suntan! Fortunately, sunbathing bored me stiff; I didn't have the patience for it. So to get that tan, I'd slather my skin with dark tan makeup. But that never worked, because all you do in Florida is sweat. I'd go to gym class and my makeup would be dripping down and white patches would materialize all over my skin.

Nowadays sunscreen (sweatproof, even!) can provide skin protection all day long. Stay away from oil-based and waterproof sunscreens on your face. It's like putting a plastic mask on your face—it doesn't let your skin sweat. Waterproof is fine for the body. Use sunscreen with an SPF of at least fifteen for good all-round protection. Ethnic skin needs sunscreen as well, as it sunburns even more than Caucasian skin. (Dark skin attracts more UV rays than white skin.) But dark skin has an advantage over white skin: It is denser, and this density acts as an aging deterrent.

The Best-Kept Secret in Skin Care

The latest buzzword in skin care, alpha-hydroxy acids (AHAs), are naturally occurring fruit acids that have been scientifically shown to improve the appearance of skin and soften fine wrinkles by sloughing off, or exfoliating, dead skin.

The best place to buy quality AHAs at reasonable prices? A dermatologist's office. Many dermatologists make their own brands of creams and cleansers or carry nationally distributed brands like NeoStrata. It's almost a trade secret that you can buy these products without a prescription or an appointment—just walk in and ask for them. These doctor-formulated products are highly pure, and since you apply only a small amount, last a long time. (See the Resource Guide at the back of the book for telephone numbers of recommended brands.)

Glycolic peels are usually performed by a qualified doctor in the office and do a great job getting rid of dead skin cells—and exfoliating dead skin is what it's all about in skin care. Even moisturizer can't penetrate dead skin cells.

Cleaning Up

The stress of modern-day living can take its toll on the skin, and time is precious. I know it is for me. So, with the help of aesthetician and makeup artist Cassandra Scott and nationally renowned dermatologist Dr. Forrest C. Brown, I've developed a skin care routine that can be done simply, quickly, and inexpensively. The most important thing you can do on a regular basis is exfoliate dead skin cells. Men do this every day when they shave. Look for exfoliating cleansers and lotions in drugstores and department store makeup counters.

Note that the skin care routines for each skin type are similar. The cosmetics industry has created a market for new products by breaking down skin types, which really aren't all that different. In general, stay away from oil-based products. Cleanse your skin with a neutral, pH-balanced cleanser like Cetaphil, or ask your dermatologist to recommend one. If you regularly exfoliate and feed your skin moisture, your skin condition will become balanced and normal within a month.

Normal Skin

Normal skin is a great gift. Normal skin is good-textured, fine-grained, clear, translucent, smooth, and slightly moist. It's flexible and soft, with a pH of 5.6–7. My skin is normal to dry, and this is my daily skin care regimen.

A.M. Skin Care

1. Cleanse with cleansing milk or cleansing emulsion. Use a terry cloth.
2. Tone using freshener with cotton balls.
3. Apply moisturizer and include eye area.
4. Then I like to feed my skin with emulsions A, C, and E (find in health food stores).

P.M. Skin Care

1. I cleanse and tone much the same as I do in the morning. I always remove the eye makeup first.
2. Then I like to spritz on a little Evian. The water draws the moisturizers into the pores.
3. I apply a light coating of a capsule of vitamin E oil or plain old baby oil.
4. Finally, I put on a face cream.

I exfoliate my face three times a week in the evening. I use a moisturizer mask once a week after cleansing and exfoliating. I apply the moisture mask and then I shower, which allows the steam to set and add moisture to the mask.

Dry Skin

Dry skin is often flaky or scaly. It is delicate in texture, thin, and can be blotchy and have brown spots. Fair-skinned people often have dry skin. Dry skin feels tight and may be itchy. It also reacts to sun and wind exposure more than normal or oily. Dry skin may have a tendency to show early fine lines. pH 0–4.

A.M. Skin Care

1. Cleanse with cleansing milk or cleansing emulsion. Use a terry cloth.
2. Tone with nonalcoholic freshener with cotton balls.
3. Apply moisturizer and include eye area.
4. Feed skin with vitamins A, C, and E.

P.M. Skin Care

1. Cleanse and tone much the same as you do in the morning.
2. Then spritz on a little Evian. The water draws the moisturizers into the pores.
3. Apply a light coating of a capsule of vitamin E oil or plain old baby oil.
4. Put on a face cream.

Exfoliate three times a week in the evening. Use a moisturizer mask once a week after cleansing and exfoliating. Apply the moisture mask and then shower, which allows the steam to set and add moisture to the mask.

Oily Skin

Oily skin is coarse, thick, and rough-textured, with large pores. It can look greasy or shiny. Makeup does not stay on well on oily skin, which often has a dull, sluggish appearance, with surface scaliness. The skin may break out in blackheads, blotches, pimples, or cysts. Oily skin is more likely to occur in olive-complexioned individuals. pH 9–14.

A.M. *Skin Care*

1. Cleanse with a neutral gel cleanser. Use a terry cloth.
2. Tone with a nonalcoholic freshener with cotton balls.
3. Oily skin needs moisturizer, too.
4. Feed skin with products that contain vitamins A and E.

P.M. *Skin Care*

1. Cleanse with an exfoliating product three times a week at night.
2. Spritz on a little Evian. The water draws the moisturizers into the pores.
3. Put on a face cream.

Combination Skin

Combination skin is dry around the eyes, cheeks, and neck; and oily around the forehead, nose, and chin (referred to as the "T-zone"). This skin type may also suffer from dilated pores, blackheads, or pimples. Combination skin seems to be the most common skin type. It's caused by an irregular distribution of glandular oils, causing enlarged pores and blackheads in the oily area, or T-zone, and dry, flaky skin in the dry zone. The skin is slightly coarse and sallow. pH 0–4; T-zone ph 9–14. The trick is to lubricate dry areas and neutralize oily areas.

A.M. *Skin Care*

1. Cleanse with a neutral cleanser over the entire face. Use a terry cloth.
2. Tone with a freshener on the T-zone only.

3. Apply moisturizer to the dry areas.
4. Then feed skin with vitamins A, E, and C.

P.M. *Skin Care*

1. Use an exfoliation masque three times a week.
2. Moisturize entire face with a water-based moisturizer.

Delta's A.M. Makeup Regimen

My makeup routine has gotten simpler and simpler—and that reflects my busy life and time spent doing the really important things. For me, the routine depends on which Delta I need to be that day—just me goofing around, or Delta Burke, Celebrity, making an appearance.

Delta Tip: Before you start, you may want to invest in those nifty little foam-rubber cosmetic sponges (found in drugstores; they come already cut up or you can cut them up yourself), cotton balls, and makeup brushes. My big splurge is on good makeup brushes. But you don't have to buy expensive designer brushes. Instead of paying top dollar for cosmetic brushes, visit an art supply or crafts store, where sable brushes are sold in most any size you need. They work beautifully and are priced right.

When I wear makeup, I keep my daytime version natural and light.

1. I start by applying a moisturizer with sunscreen as a base to dual-finish powder.
2. Then I apply a natural-tone under-eye cream concealer.
3. My cool skin tones work well with mauve hues in both blush and lipstick. For a natural day look, I apply just a few brushes of blush on the apple of my cheek. Blending is very important in every step of makeup

application. I blend the blush in well with a small cosmetic sponge. Then I follow the natural shape of my lip with a mauve lipstick.

4. People often say that my most striking feature are my blue eyes. So I play them up. For day, I use an eyeshadow brush to sweep a mauve-toned powder blush (the same I use on my cheeks) over the eyelid and under the eyebrow. Then I blend it in with a small sponge.

5. I'm lucky to have naturally long, black lashes, so for day I simply use one coat of black mascara on my top lashes and a quick short coat on my bottom lashes.

6. For my brow, I follow the brow line with clear mascara.

7. Finally, I like to blend around the jawline with a cosmetic sponge to ensure that there are no tell-tale lines showing.

Total time: 10–15 minutes.

Delta's P.M. Megawatt Glamour Regimen

I pull out all the stops with my on-set glamour makeup routine, for that extra-special evening. Because the lighting at night is softer and more forgiving, you can experiment with more dramatic looks. Before you begin, set the mood. Put on some soothing music. Take a bubble bath. Light some candles. You'll feel as beautiful as you look.

1. I start with under-eye concealer one shade lighter than my skin tone.

2. I apply a cream foundation to my face, blending down past the jawline and into the neck.

3. I then set the foundation or base with loose powder, applied with a brush or a cotton ball. (Be sure to blow any excess powder off the brush before you apply it.)

1
5
7

For evening I use a powder with a slight pink tint. Women with warm skin tones may want to use a yellow-based product.

4. With a contour brush, I brush a light brown contour powder gently onto a small area directly under the cheek line in an upward motion. I do the same along the jawline and under the chin. Use a powder brush to remove excess powder. Then I use a small cosmetic sponge to smudge and blend all contour lines. Sometimes I'll put a little corrective contouring on the sides of my nose.

5. I like to add a dab of mauve blush to the apples of the cheek, after which I feather the blush upward just a little.

6. I follow my natural lip line with a freshly sharpened rose-colored lip pencil. With a Q-Tip I feather the lip pencil just slightly into the body of the lips. I then use the lip pencil to fill in the major portion of the bottom lip. Again, I like a mauve-colored lipstick, which I apply from the tube or with a lip brush. Then I set the lipstick with a tissue, maybe even dusting loose powder over the tissue beforehand. For a pouty look I sometimes add a little lip gloss to the very center of the bottom lip.

7. I don't like to get powder on my lashes. That's why I apply eye shadow before I use mascara. I use a matte medium-brown on the eyelid. I apply with a brush to the center of the lid and feather the shadow out and up.

8. To play up the small golden flecks in the iris of my eyes, I like to apply a matte yellow powder shadow from the inner corner of my eye and feather it outward.

9. If I'm really going all out, I'll apply a gray or a burgundy matte powder shadow to accent the eye crease. This is also done with a shadow brush. Following the natural bone structure of my eye, I again feather the powder out and up.

10. Directly under the brow line I dab a small amount of beige or off-white cream shadow with a cosmetic sponge and then blend it with my fingertips. For a shimmery effect, set with a slightly iridescent powder.

11. I then use a brow powder in a dark brown and follow the natural shape of my brow line. You can even set your brow line with clear mascara. Sometimes, to create the illusion of depth, I like to apply individual lashes on the outer corners of my eye. After the glue has dried, I line the top lashes with a charcoal liner. I like the cake or pen type, and draw the line as close to the natural lash as possible. This line is then smudged over with a matching powder. Lower lashes are sometimes lined as well, but with a thinner line and then smudged over with a burgundy powder. For a soft, natural look, blend the harsh lines of the liners several times.

12. Finally, I curl my lashes gently. I apply black or midnight-blue mascara—two coats for a really smashing evening.

Total time: 30–45 minutes.

The Busy Woman's Ten-Minute A.M. Routine

I think this routine clocks in at less than ten minutes.

1. Apply a light coat of matte eyeshadow.
2. Apply a light coat of eyeliner.
3. Apply one coat of mascara.
4. Apply a light coating of blush with a brush.
5. Apply matte lipstick.

The Busy Woman's Ten-Minute P.M. Routine

When Mac comes home and says, "I'm taking you out to dinner. Can you be ready in ten minutes?" I take my ten-minute A.M. routine a couple of steps farther.

1. I apply a second coat of mascara.
2. I apply an opalescent eye shadow over the matte shadow for a shimmery nighttime effect.
3. I apply a glossy coat of lipstick over the matte.

Delta's Home Spa: Miracle Fruits for the Face

Women of size deserve pampering just as much as any other woman. The good news is, you don't have to look far to find some of the most effective skin care products in the world. You will get amazing results from natural skin care treats that you whip up at home using ordinary items from your kitchen—for mere pennies. Did you know, for example, that leftover bananas and strawberries make a great moisturizing masque? That milk acids are good too? That's why buttermilk is so good for the skin.

Women throughout time have known the benefits of these age-old formulas. But scientists are now beginning to understand why. Homemade fruit concoctions replicate glycolic formulas, which are alpha-hydroxy acids made from sugarcane.

The following easy-to-make fruit and vegetable concoctions for the face are the creations of Cassandra Scott and Dr. Forrest Brown. Keep in mind that because fresh fruits are natural sources of alpha-hydroxy acids, it is important to moisturize after each treatment to help keep skin soft and hydrated.

Please note: In preparing these beauty potions, Cassandra advises that you avoid using metal if possible. The vitamins in these fruits and vegetables are so perishable that some are lost on contact with metal. If I mention alcohol in any of these concoctions, it must be pure grain alcohol, which is hard to get—try a health food store or pharmacy. If you can't find it, substitute distilled water, but then double the steeping time for flowers or herbs.

Also, be sure to use plastic strainers or spatulas when blending, whipping, or pureeing. Try not to use tap water; it's preferable to use distilled water if any water is required.

Apricot Moisturizing Masque

This is a great moisturizing treatment for dry skin.

Soak **dried apricots** in **warm water** in a closed jar. When the water has cooled, refrigerate the solution for twenty-four hours. Then mash the apricots in the same liquid, using a wooden or plastic spatula. Apply the pack to the face and leave on for twenty minutes. Rinse with **tepid water.** The iron in the apricot penetrates the skin and gives a fabulous effect.

Dr. Brown's Favorite Masque for Dry Skin

Use this concoction to relieve dryness and improve the texture of the skin. It leaves the skin incredibly hydrated.

Make a puree of **banana, papaya, peach** (you might even add an **avocado**). Apply it to the skin, leave on for twenty minutes, then rinse with **tepid water.** Follow with **margarine** or **polyunsaturated oil.** Then rinse again with **tepid water.**

Cassandra's Total All-Round Beauty Masque

Note: It's important first to make sure that your skin is not irritated by strawberries. Put a little mashed strawberry on a patch of skin on your arm. Leave it there for ten minutes. If your skin becomes itchy or red, leave out the strawberries.

Take a handful of **strawberries,** a medium-ripe **banana, plain yogurt** (1 small carton), 4 tablespoons of **honey,** 1 tablespoon of **lemon juice,** 1 tablespoon of **orange juice,** and a cup of **oatmeal.**

Blend in a blender or food processor with a plastic blade until mixed but not liquefied. On moist, cleansed skin, apply to the neck, chest, and face area, avoiding the eye area. Slice a chilled **cucumber** and place the slices over your eyes. Put a cool cloth over your eyes. Lie down, elevate your feet, put on some music, and try to have someone nearby to massage your feet. If not, pretend that there is. Lie peacefully for fifteen minutes. Slowly get up and remove the masque with **tepid water.** You'll feel refreshed, revitalized, and beautiful.

Delta's Fresh Fruit Lotion
I use this lotion when I'm on the road and tired and feel my skin is dehydrated.

Mix a little **orange juice** or **half orange and grapefruit juice** with **fresh milk** or **distilled water.** (I prefer the fresh milk.) Bathe it on the face, leaving it there for three to five minutes. Rinse it off for soft, glowing skin.

Honey Masque
Honey is an antiseptic, a stimulant, and good for dry skin.

Heat some **honey** until it is manageable. Apply it to the entire neck and face, including the area around the eyes. Allow it to remain on the face from ten to fifteen minutes. Then remove with **tepid water.**

Lemon Milk Lotion for Wrinkles
This is a wonderful moisturizing lotion.

Cover a slice of **lemon** with **milk.** Allow it to steep for two hours. Strain and apply the solution over the face area. Let it dry, then wash it off with **olive oil.**

Mayonnaise Facial
This treatment softens rough, scaly skin.

Massage warm **mayonnaise** (not Miracle Whip) into the

skin. Leave on the skin for fifteen minutes and then rinse thoroughly with **tepid water.**

Milk of Magnesia Pack
This is a great pack to help clear up oily-skin breakouts.

Pour a tablespoon of **milk of magnesia** into your palm and apply to skin; leave it on for twenty minutes. Remove with **tepid water.**

Milk-Herb Moisturizer Toner
This toner can be made ahead and kept in the refrigerator to use when you need it; it keeps for a week. It has a wonderful moisturizing, astringent, and healing effect.

Steep **sage, mint,** and/or **carnations** in hot water. Keep in a cool place for twenty-four hours. Drain and mix in a little **sweet cream, butter,** or **milk.** Apply to face. Keep in fridge no more than a week. Use daily as you like.

Tomato Masque
Use to combat large pores or oily or problem skin.

Mash a **tomato** until it's pulpy. Apply it to face, especially around the large-pore area. The vitamins, minerals, and acids in the tomato have an astringent effect. Rinse with **tepid water.**

Wheat Germ Masque
This masque works wonders for oily or sensitive skin.

Mix together 1 tablespoon of **wheat germ powder** and 1 tablespoon of **plain yogurt.** Apply to the skin and leave on for fifteen minutes. Rinse with **tepid water.**

Yogurt Masque
This treatment soothes and relieves inflamed, blemished skin.

Apply **plain yogurt** lightly over the face. Leave it on for half an hour. Remove with **tepid water. Sour cream** or **buttermilk** can be substituted for the yogurt.

Natural Solutions

Tired, Puffy, Irritated, or Swollen Eyes
Steep a **teabag** in hot water. Put in the refrigerator to cool. Apply it as a compress to the eyes.

Eye Allergies
Eye allergies are a universal problem. Many actors suffer eye allergies when filming on location in a new climate. Soak absorbent pads in cold **nonfat milk.** Apply the pads over the eyes for ten minutes twice a day. It really helps relieve eye allergies.

Sunburn
Mash a couple of fresh **tomatoes** (or **cucumbers**) and mix with **buttermilk.** Apply to sunburned area. It helps relieve the pain and can turn sunburn into tan with less peeling involved. If we're smart, we won't have sunburn, right? Use your sunscreen.

Freckles or Age Spots
Lighten discolored areas by dabbing **lemon juice** on the areas daily, followed by a moisturizer. Don't rub it into the skin; the juice can be irritating.

Problems and How to Solve Them

Small Eyes
To bring out small eyes, use a light-colored eye shadow.

Prominent Eyes
To make prominent eyes look smaller, use a dark-colored eye shadow.

Wide Nose

Use a darker color foundation or darker powder in the same hue as your regular foundation, and apply with a cosmetic sponge on the sides of nose. Set with powder and blend.

Double Chin

Use contour powder underneath the chin and blend, blend, blend. You don't want a line showing.

Round Cheeks

If you want to show some definition in your cheekbones, use contour powder or blush underneath the cheek. For a natural, healthy look, smile and brush the blush on the apple of the cheeks. Blend.

Under-Eye Bags

Under-eye bags or circles are hereditary or are caused by sinus problems, vitamin deficiencies, or lack of sleep. Use a combination yellow- and green-toned concealer that is one shade lighter than your skin tone and blend. Follow with your facial foundation.

Hollywood Tricks of the Trade

- If your cream foundation is too heavy for daytime wear, add a little moisturizer to the makeup—not water; it makes makeup look streaky. Using your finger or a cosmetic sponge, apply to face.
- Use clear mascara on the brow line to set the brow color.
- Have your eyelashes dyed. It's incredibly inexpensive and safe, as long as you make sure to have it done by a trained technician in a reliable salon. Then, in the morning, you simply curl them or apply a coat of clear mascara. The effect lasts six weeks.

- For a pouty look, add a little iridescent eye shadow or lip gloss to the very center of the bottom lip.
- Use a dollop of hair gel to keep brows in place.
- Turn your blemish into a beauty mark. Cover it with light to medium brown eyeliner and set it with powder.
- To get that false eyelashes look, apply one coat of mascara, cover the lashes with powder, then apply another coat. Let dry and separate lashes with a metal eyelash comb.
- To make lipstick stay forever, first line the lips with lip liner. Then put the lip liner all over the lips and smooth it with your finger. Finally, put your lipstick on.
- Always round the bow of your lips, never make the bow pointy.
- To cover up a blemish, use a yellow-toned concealer.

Makeup Hit List

1. Keep your equipment clean. Recycle cosmetic sponges by soaking used sponges in hot, soapy water. Clean your brushes with mild shampoo.
2. Blend! Whether using cream foundation, contour powder, or blush, blending goes a long way in creating a seamless, natural look. Smudging and blending prevent harsh divisions of color on your face.
3. Throw away mascara that is more than three months old or that irritates your eyes.
4. Never share eye makeup. Bacteria can easily spread from person to person and cause an eye infection.
5. The most important item to spend money on is foundation. Film-set makeup artists love dual-finish makeup powder, which provides nice coverage and stays on all day, and the matte powder goes on like both a powder and a cream.

CHAPTER 5

Big Hair

Big Hair: Closer to God

I like Big Hair. It makes me feel powerful. When I lived in Hollywood, the only car that would fit me *and* my hair was a jumbo-size Jeep. So there I'd be, at openings and appearances, all done up in pink chiffon, high heels, and Big Hair and struggling out of that Jeep.

I like to say that having Big Hair brings me closer to God. I have a standing joke with my

favorite hairstylist, Virginia Kearns. No matter how she styles my hair, when she's done I always ask her if my hair is big enough. We just look at each other and laugh and start singing "Just a Closer Walk with Thee."

Sometimes when my Latin look kicks in, Big Hair gets so big I have to stick accessories in it just to keep it from taking over my body. I'll use falls, ribbons—you name it—just to break it up so it doesn't look like a Christmas tree without any ornaments. I love adding wigs and hairpieces. I believe I can safely say that I was the only student at Colonial High who would wear a wig to class.

There have been times lately, however, when even for me, my hair has gotten too big. Maybe that means I don't need such big hair to feel powerful. If it's too big, I end up feeling silly . . .

66 . . . *which has never stopped you before. I only say this because I envy hair, big, little, or medium.* **99** —Gerald McRaney

If I want *really* Big Hair, here's my routine. After washing and conditioning my hair, I blow it dry with a little mousse applied to the ends. Then I use setting lotion and hot rollers to curl it. Then I tease the heck out of it. With my head hanging over, I spray my hair with hair spray. When I come up, there's the Big Hair. I then simply shape it the way I want it.

Big Hair makes sense in my business: It's bigger than life, over the top, attention getting—all the things that a big ham like me gets up in the morning for. But it also makes sense, proportion-wise, for a real-size woman like me.

Hair and the Real-Size Woman

As my friend and hairstylist Virginia Kearns tells me, a large-size body tends to make the head look smaller and therefore somewhat out of proportion. Your hair should complement

In preparation for the Miss America pageant, pageant officials insisted on a makeover. I got my eyebrows plucked and my makeup turned up a notch or two—and was first introduced to Big Hair. Miss Florida Pagent

and balance your entire look—not just the face. Most real-size women need some volume to balance the proportion. Hair that is full and high can be a flattering look for real-size ladies.

Take a snowman, for example. If you just put eyes, nose, and a mouth on him he still looks round. But if you put a hat on top of his head, then he doesn't look quite so round and he picks up his own personality. For real-size women, a cut that is short and flat to the head can look out of proportion; the head appears too small for the body.

With that said, I still believe that the bottom line in hairstyle—and in *any* style—is personal choice. Oh, there are many theories on the most flattering hairstyles for real-size women, and many are based in solid, commonsense reasoning. Some people seem to think if your face is heavy, then you should keep hair away from the face. Or that you should cut it short to sleeken the face and emphasize the neck. Just remember to *keep the style soft*. Don't try to pull it back in a twist unless you leave some tendrils hanging softly around the face or neck area. Even if you just pull it into a ponytail, leave some softness around the face.

Use the following style suggestions as a guide to find the look you're happiest with. Your crowning glory should please *you* first and foremost.

Round Face

If your face is round, you may want to slenderize or elongate it. To do that, you lift the top. If you want to wear your hair down, leave the back down and pull the sides up with combs or barrettes—it's amazing how doing something that simple can change the whole look. Bangs or a part lengthens a round face as well. If you want to pull your hair up, let a few tendrils hang down to soften the effect.

Square Face

On a square face it is better to leave some—if not all—hair

Big, Big Hollywood Hair. I was playing a villainess on <u>Fantasy Island</u>. Can you tell? Collection of Delta Burke

down to soften the sharp jawline. If you pull your hair tight off your face, people will see that square jaw and think, There goes stubbornness personified. However, if you bring hair forward to softly cover your square jaw, you will look soft all over. It's a good idea not to cut your hair above your chin line. Even a pageboy is a good style for a square face, because once again it covers the sides of the jaw with soft simplicity. Another easy way to soften any harsh lines in the face: Simply feather your hair forward.

Oval Face

An oval face responds to many different styles. The face is naturally elongated just by the shape. Once again, however, you want your hairstyle to provide softness around the face and neck. It's all about making your head a size to equal your body. I am a very firm believer in the fact that short, short hair looks good only on beanpoles. Because they are so thin they need to make their head look smaller to match the proportion of their body to their head. Rarely does a real-size lady need to make her head smaller. If you pull the sides up, do them softly, not tight. Just a slight puff on the sides can soften the face beyond words. Or leave a couple of tendrils down and floating around to update the look. The eye will go to the soft tendrils before catching the severeness of the hairdo.

Delta's Wash-and-Go Styles

66 *However I fix her hair, Delta's style comes from inside Delta. She's real people and absolutely wonderful inside and out. There are none better.* 99   —Virginia Kearns

In my pageant days, I learned a trick or two about hair. One of my favorite tricks solved the problem of wearing a crown. I'd go to a hairstylist with crown in tow, and—if I was wearing them—any hairpieces, and have my hair styled around the crown. Then I'd get home and wrap toilet paper around the whole thing, holding it fast with bobby pins, and sleep in it. I'd wake up in the morning, remove the tissue and pins, and go

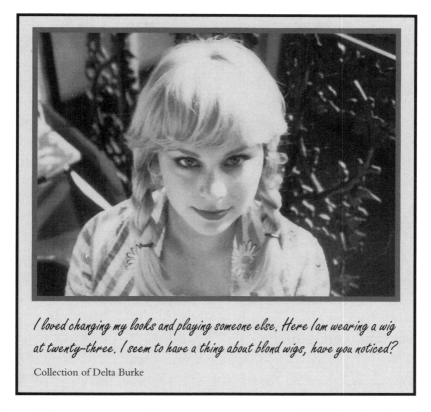

I loved changing my looks and playing someone else. Here I am wearing a wig at twenty-three. I seem to have a thing about blond wigs, have you noticed?

Collection of Delta Burke

straight to a personal appearance, crown and hairdo firmly in place. Perfect hair every time, thanks to my mother and grandmother, who used this trick in their beehive-hairdo days.

That kind of labor-intensive attention to hair is no longer part of my daily routine. Easy, quick, and low-maintenance does it for me these days.

I like to wear my hair about shoulder length and off the face. Mac likes it off my neck; he likes those soft, wispy tendrils. For the style I most often wear—loose and curly—I set my hair with hot rollers. This gives me enough curl to work with. For most days, I just wear it curly all over. High on top—closer to God, remember—soft but not too full on the sides, and very full in back. It's simple but effective.

Below are some quick, attractive ways to do your hair simply for everyday wear.

Quick and Easy Curls

If your hair is stick straight and you want to give your hair lift and body without resorting to a body wave, here are several ways to do so. Shampoo your hair, apply mousse to ends, and scrunch your hair until it is almost dry. Then take a curling iron and curl the scrunch. Never use a brush on this style—it will straighten the hair shaft. Try putting up the sides of this style with combs or pins, which gives you even more height, as well as an excuse not to have to wash it every day.

Pageboy

This quick and easy hairdo can help de-emphasize a prominent jawline. Simply use a curling iron (the bigger the size of the iron, the bigger and looser the curl) and roll it forward on the sides in an up-down fashion. It will stay that way all day.

Straight and Slinky

Straight hair can help elongate a round face. If your hair is wavy, here's a quick way to make it straight. Direct the airflow of your blow-dryer down the hair shaft. Before drying the ends, add a light coating of gel or mousse. Then pull hair taut with a large brush while drying on high heat. If you want your hair even more straight, apply a defrizzing product before you dry it.

The Joan Crawford

This hairdo helps make the face look longer and thinner. Simply take your regular hairdo and pull the sides up with combs or barrettes.

The French Twist

This style, one of my favorite looks, exposes a pretty neckline. Tease your hair as high as you want—the body from teasing allows you to do far more shaping than normal.

The Home Spa: Virginia's Miracle Homemade Hair Conditioners

Virginia Kearns has worked in the movie and television business for more than twenty-five years. She is an Emmy-winning hairstylist who has worked on long-running TV shows—including *Hill Street Blues* and *Taxi*—as well as major motion pictures and soap operas. So she knows of what she speaks. Here are the recipes for three of her favorite hair-care treatments, recipes that were previously considered trade secrets. I use them all religiously.

Mayonnaise Conditioner

Find a day when you have nothing planned except housework. Take a jar of **mayonnaise** and slather it all over your hair. Wrap a plastic bag around your hair, secure it with a hinged clip, and forget about it. Vacuum, scrub, work, pay bills, do whatever you have to do—just leave the mayonnaise in all day. The protein from the egg soaks into your hair, adding strength, and the oil in the mayonnaise tames split ends. It's a wonderful conditioner and less expensive than store-bought ones. Pamper yourself with the mayonnaise conditioner once a month.

Oil and Pepper Hair Revitalizer

Mix a pinch of **cayenne pepper** into a quarter cup to a half cup of **olive oil.** Put this mixture on your hair, wrap it up in plastic, and leave it up all day. Be sure to keep the cayenne mixture away from the eye area. The oil conditions the hair much like the mayonnaise, and the cayenne works to stimulate the scalp—sometimes to the point of new hair growth, much like peach fuzz. It's simple but very effective. Plus it is all natural, and not as hard to wash out of the hair as you may think!

Beer Rinse for Oily Hair

Beer really cuts the grease in oily hair and leaves hair soft and shiny. Simply take a can of **beer** out of the refrigerator and let it sit until it is room temperature. Then wash your hair as normal and use the beer as a rinse. The odor will be gone as soon as your hair dries.

Hair Dos and Don'ts

Don't take your hair for granted. It is your crowning glory. It helps keep you warm in winter and cool in summer. It protects your scalp from the damaging effects of the sun. It is one of your most malleable features. You can shape it to make a personal statement, transform your look, or simply lift your spirits.

A good haircut is half the battle; it makes the care and tending of hair so much easier. You'll know you've got a good cut if it keeps its shape as it grows out and is easy to style. If a cut is a shoddy one, you'll know it in three to four weeks, when the cut basically falls apart and becomes hard to manage and doesn't hold its shape.

DON'T brush wet hair. It will break it and give you split ends. When hair is wet, it has a tendency to stretch, but pulling on that stretched hair is asking for trouble.

DO use a comb or a pick gently to comb out wet hair.

DON'T brush hair from the root down. It is extremely hard on the hair. If the hair has been teased even a little, it is like pulling the hair out by the root—and it hurts. Forcing those tangles will pull the hair to the breaking point and snap it off like a rope with frayed edges.

DO brush from the bottom up, so that by the time you reach the scalp, the tangles will slide out.

DON'T use a superhot dryer on your hair. This will give

you frizzy ends faster than pulling it wet with a brush.

DO use a warm or cool setting—your hair will dry just as fast—and hold the dryer well away from your head.

DON'T use a dryer directly on permed or naturally curly hair.

DO use a diffuser attachment, which actually diffuses the hot air from the dryer so that it doesn't hit the hair directly. If you want to straighten your hair, dry it partway with the diffuser then pull it straight with a round brush.

DON'T give up on coarse, thick hair.

DO set it with end papers and rollers, and your style will keep beautifully until the next shampoo.

DON'T give up on fine, straight hair.

DO brush it frequently and trim it every six weeks. It will look fuller if you tip your head over to brush air into it. Fine, straight hair looks much fuller if you keep it blunt cut.

DON'T expose frizzy hair to hot dryers.

DO use a leave-in conditioner each time you shampoo and moist heat to straighten or curl it. Steam rollers are perfect for frizzy hair. Try some of the new antifrizz products as well to see what works best for you.

DON'T use the same shampoo over and over again.

DO keep two or three different shampoos in your shower so you can switch frequently so that your hair doesn't become accustomed to one product and it loses some of its effectiveness. Try switching products once a month. If you use gel or mousse daily, then you need to find a shampoo that removes buildup.

DON'T leave short hair flat.

DO blow it dry for height. If you wear short hair flat against your head, it will resemble a ball sitting on your shoulders. But if you blow it dry, with your head upside down to get some air into it, then your head will more naturally be in proportion with your body size. Remember: *Very* few people can wear their hair short and flat.

DON'T go swimming without protecting your hair first.

DO wear a swim cap. Otherwise, apply conditioner to your hair before you go in the water. Reapply each time you go back in. Rinse with clear water as soon as you get out of the pool. And use shampoo specially designed to remove chlorine.

Hollywood Tricks of the Trade

- If you use a lot of hair spray and you're afraid to brush your hair out for fear of breaking it, try sprinkling a little baking soda on it. Baking soda breaks up the spray—and costs pennies.
- Use a butane curling iron for quick touch-ups. These come in various sizes and shapes to give you the look you want. Hollywood stylists keep one handy at all times on the set to instantly make a curl tighter or hair straighter between shots.
- For very thin, fine hair, style it by stuffing it. It sounds silly, but it works. A product found in most beauty supply shops, called crepe wool, comes in lengths that look like a braid. You can stretch it and pull it apart and do almost anything with it—including literally stuffing it into your hair to create a French roll or a bun. It also comes in colors very close to your own and you can mix them to get them closer to your color.
- At a wig store, buy what is called wefts. This is human hair that is sewn in one long line so that you can cut it to fit your head. Wig shops also sell the clips you can sew on

to hook it into your hair. Most of them can be dyed to match your hair color. Take your wefts to your favorite stylist and have him or her show you some different ways to use it.

- If you want to hold your hair back, say, with a decorative comb, take a bobby pin and slightly bend it, then put in hair to hold hair and comb in place all day.
- Don't overcondition hair if you want to curl it. Gloppy conditioners make hair too slippery to curl. The easiest hair to curl? Clean, freshly washed, and dried.
- Day-old hair has more body to work with and is easily reset or recurled into a different style.
- Rinse your hair with cool water rather than hot; it gives hair a smooth, shiny glow.

Real-Size Secret Weapon: Color

Because of my lifelong Marilyn Monroe fixation, I have always coveted blond hair. As a teenager my arsenal of wigs included a couple of blond jobs; one I wore playing Cherie in *Bus Stop,* a role Marilyn made famous. When I worked on *The Seekers,* I came to the set in a blond wig that I never took off. During the entire shoot, the crew had no clue that I was a brunette. Of course, I went blond all the way in *Delta,* when I felt I needed a lift, a sunny change in my life. And for a while, it did just that. But then I realized I needed to work from the inside out.

The amazing thing about being adventurous with your hair is that it can have an immediate, positive effect on your attitude. For real-size women, going with a lighter, brighter color is also a great way to soften and lighten the face. It brightens the skin tone—and even thickens thin hair.

Before you do anything drastic, do your homework. The color of your hair should match your complexion and your eyes. Most colorists say you should stay within two to three shades of your natural color. If you have an olive skin tone, for

The blond sex kitten at eighteen, with kitten. Collection of Delta Burke

example, gray-blond hair won't do. When I went blond, I knew right away it wouldn't be a long-term change. My pale complexion is a natural match for my dark brown hair.

The best way to find a hair color that works well with your skin tones and eye color is to try on some wigs. Before you make the plunge, make sure you:

1. Take the color of your eyebrows into account and make sure the new hair color isn't too much of a contrast with your brow shade.
2. Notice what the new hair color does for your eyes.
3. Think about your current wardrobe. Picture in your mind the colors you most often wear and whether a

new hair color translates into footing the bill for a whole new set of clothes.

4. Consider the cost and upkeep. Single-process hair coloring—coloring the entire head of hair—reveals darker roots sooner than, say, painting highlights on random strips of hair. Highlighting needs to be retouched only every two to six months. Single-process hair coloring will probably need a retouch to the roots every four to six weeks.

5. Consider gray hair. Nature will eventually lighten your hair with gray. If your gray is coming in too fast, highlight your hair. Have lighter colors woven in. When done right, it looks completely natural, like sunlit hair.

6. Remember that hair color fades and that the shampoo you use can either perk it up or dull it out. Look for shampoos made especially for colored hair; they won't strip the color from your hair.

7. Know the natural way to brighten the color. Use a lemon rinse to make blond highlights shine and a vinegar rinse to brighten brunette hair. For the first, squeeze a whole lemon into a cup of water and apply to just-washed hair. Lemon is very acidic and will help to lighten the hair. Rinse out. To brighten brunette hair, put 2 or 3 tablespoons of vinegar into a cup of water and apply to just-washed hair. Rinse out. The vinegar odor will vanish as soon as your hair dries.

8. Reconsider going darker. Generally, dark dyes can look fake and can also make you look older.

9. Give yourself or have a salon give you a deep conditioner along with the hair coloring to minimize the damage that any chemical processing—whether coloring or a perm—will do to your hair. On the other hand, the processing coats the hair shaft and makes it thicker and gives it more body, great for people with fine, thin hair.

10. Get a consultation from a hair care professional before you do anything.

I wore a blond wig during the entire filming of <u>The Seekers</u>. None of the crew had a clue that I was really a brunette——I got to work before everyone else to have this wig glued to my head. Photofest (<u>The Seekers</u>)

No wigs this time: I went blond all the way for my sitcom Delta. Greg Gorman

Optimistic Shopping

As a world-class shopper, I have become a collector by necessity. In my possession I have collections of antique quilts, vintage lockets, stiletto-heeled shoes, wide-brimmed hats, old fabrics, Victorian jewelry—even antique clothing patterns. But that's not all. Every travel souvenir, every theme-park tchotchke, every tacky plastic collectible, I collect. It's a habit I'm working to curtail. I was so proud of myself when I recently

visited Niagara Falls and did not buy one thing. Not one magnet, not one mug, not one place mat. I was sorely tempted, though, because acquiring things is one of my guilty pleasures.

My best friend, Lucia, and her daughter, Cory, at my second wedding. I designed the flower girl outfits—they even had pantaloons—and all their accessories. Collection of Delta Burke

❝ *The first year of* **Designing Women,** *Harry [Thomason] and I took Delta to Arkansas for a benefit. Everyone there fell in love with her, and she bought out every store in town. We dined at one of the neighboring plantations, and she tried to buy that too.* **❞** —Linda Bloodworth-Thomason

When I was so unhappy with my weight, however, the pleasure went out of shopping for clothes for me. I felt awkward and unattractive, and trying on clothes in front of a store mirror and a salesclerk with attitude only reinforced those negative feelings. I started avoiding clothing stores altogether.

It didn't help that when I did look for something to wear, I found that store owners thought so little of women of size that they offered only drab, uninspiring garments—and then stuck them down in store basements or way in the back of the store on a couple of rickety racks. Clothes of limited choices and limited colors and limited designs—and even those were hard to find.

For the thirty-six million American women who are size 14 and over, shopping for something stylish and attractive to wear has traditionally been an exercise in frustration. But no more: The market for plus-size clothing is booming, and sales are growing twice as fast as the sales of other apparel. That makes us a force to be reckoned with.

As a force, we have power in the marketplace. There is no longer a need to feel ashamed, to hide, or to play it safe. So get out there and shop for all the right reasons—because it makes you feel good, because it makes you think positive things, because it inspires you. I call it optimistic shopping.

Shopping for Value

My husband finds it amusing that I am offering advice on shopping for value. The old Delta, the one with the Grand House in

Los Angeles, used to just waltz into any old store and say, Give me that and that and that. I am now working on decluttering my life, however. It's not easy. It's very against my nature. In this respect, Mac has been an excellent influence on me.

❝ *We'd go into an antiques store, and if Delta saw something she liked, she'd just say, 'I'll take it.' No haggling, no negotiating. I'd gently draw her aside and say, 'Honey, you can't do it that way. They don't even* **expect** *you to do it that way.' When Delta goes shopping, she always needs to take along someone to lead her out of the store.* **❞** —Gerald McRaney

The number-one rule, then, may be that if shopping is your weakness, *find a shopping companion to lead you out of the store before you do any real damage.* Also keep in mind that an army of marketing forces has spent millions on ways to seduce you into buying their clothes. Don't be seduced: Remember why you are there and don't let a store's flashy bells and whistles tempt you into throwing your money away. I've heard every sales pitch in the book. In my recent attempts to declutter my life and cut back on freewheeling spending, I have found that the following suggestions can really help transform former spendaholics, like myself, into smart shoppers.

Buy for the Long Run

Go to the stores that sell goods at your price level, but if you like something and it works, don't wait for it to go on sale to purchase it. Getting a good deal on clothing is smart shopping, but how many of those "bargains" hang in your closet and are never worn? Remember too that shopping for bargains can be time-consuming, and time is money. A piece of clothing is worth the money if it is a staple for you. For example, boots are a staple of my wardrobe; I wear them with leggings, with skirts, on the farm. So if I find a pair of boots that look good and fit well, I won't wait till they're on the bargain table before buying them. I know I will get my money's worth of use.

Invest in Building Blocks for Your Wardrobe

Pinpoint your interests. Look for pieces that will serve as the foundations of your wardrobe, garments that can be used in a variety of ways and can cross over to other seasons. Never spend a lot of money for trendy, flash-in-the-pan clothing. Invest instead in garments in classic styles, durable fabrics, and neutral colors. Then simply build and accessorize around them.

Buy Clothing to Wear Now

Stop buying things only to pitch them into a "when-I-lose-ten-pounds" pile. Incentives are great, but don't deny yourself the pleasure of wearing the things you like—now. Buy the things that fit you today.

Don't Be Fooled by "Hanger Appeal"

Lots of clothes look great on a hanger but don't look good on the body, and vice versa. Always try them on.

Do Fashion-Show "Homework"

Most major department stores in large urban areas host regular fashion shows for real-size women. Call the stores in your community for a schedule. You can get a good idea of how a garment fits and moves at these shows, which feature real-size models. You can also pick up new ways to use the clothes you already own and glean tips on sewing new styles.

Washability

Wash-and-wear clothes make sense for the busy homemaker and working girl, plus you save money on dry-cleaning bills.

Know Your Body

Find the right fit and then match it to the type of clothes you like to wear.

Be Comfortable

Fit is not just about proper proportion; it's about having a garment move with you, not fight you every step of the way. Who wants to be encumbered or constricted in their daily regimen? Don't be a masochist for fashion—free yourself from the tyranny of uncomfortable clothes.

Demand More Choices

If your local department store lacks choices and new styles, make some noise. Go directly to the managers or buyers and demand better choices. Come armed with photographs and information on what's available in the marketplace. Even better: Find a group of like-minded women and go en masse.

Shopping for Fit

How can you tell if a garment is well constructed? I asked designer Barry Zelman to come up with some checkpoints to go over when considering a purchase.

1. Look for quality seaming, that is, seams sewn straight with closely spaced, tight stitching. Beware of puckering along seams. I look for princess seams, which tell me that someone has taken more time with the garment. Princess seams fit the body better and show the figure in a more flattering way.
2. Look over the buttonholes to be sure the stitching around the holes is neat, tight, and free of loose, dangling threads. Check out the quality of the buttons and make sure they fit into the holes with no pulling or puckering of the fabric.

3. Check out the action on the zipper and make sure it is concealed by fabric when it is zipped up.

4. Make sure hems are cleanly sewn and that the fabric around them doesn't pucker. Check yourself in the mirror to test whether a hem is well concealed.

5. Shoulder pads should not be obvious. If you can clearly see their outline or if they are misshapen, chances are other people will be aware of them too. Opt for pads attached with Velcro, which can be easily moved or replaced.

6. Even the way a label is sewn in can tell you a lot about how well or how poorly something is made.

Delta Style Tip

Keep in mind that real-size clothes do not match up with the sizes of misses' clothes. A plus-size 14 is actually a misses' size 16. So when you're shopping in the misses' section, look for clothes that are approximately one size up. In addition, many misses' sizes do not match up. An 8 in one designer's size may be a 10 in another. This happens for a couple of reasons: Clothing manufacturers use different fit models, and some clothing makers actually label their garments a size lower to make the consumer think she's smaller than she is and supposedly feel better about herself.

Shopping for Vintage

I like to find things that had a past life and give them a new life. One of my favorite pieces of clothing was a vintage leopard sequin coat I found in a flea market fifteen years ago. I lived in that old coat till it got too ratty to wear. Anything vintage I love: antique fabrics, 1940s clothes, Victorian earrings, even vintage fabric. Old fabrics are beautiful, beautifully made, and long-lasting. I use them to cover seats and footstools or have vests made from them. I have a family heirloom, a 1938 chenille bedspread, that I plan to make into a robe from one of the antique clothing patterns I collect. I collect antique quilts and often have new quilts made from antique material.

Why vintage? First of all, the pieces are generally one-of-a-kind. You won't show up at a party and find everyone else wearing the same thing. Second, the price is right. You get high style and quality handiwork at bargain rates. Third, wearing a piece of cloth from another era gives you an immediate and intimate connection to the past. You wonder whose fingers adjusted the collar in front of a smoky mirror, whose eyes followed the sweep of the skirt.

Keep in mind that finding large sizes in vintage clothing can be a challenge. That's why you should pay as much attention to the men's sections at vintage shops, where classically tailored jackets and pants are in abundance, and the roomy sizes may fit you to a T. I also like to look for antique capes: They're unique, dramatic, and extravagantly sized. You may find, however, that vintage stores are most useful for the little antique collectibles and trimmings—jewelry, bags, buttons, scarves—that add so much to an outfit. I sometimes find a piece that is too faded and fragile but that has a nice lace trim or buttons I can use on another outfit. Here are a few ways to use those collectibles.

- Change the entire look of an outfit simply by replacing the buttons. Look for garments in your closet that can be revitalized by replacing plain buttons with pretty antique buttons.
- Add antique or embroidered belt loops to skirts or pants.
- Use old fabric as swashbuckling belts.
- Add lacy antique trims to your skirt or dress hems.
- Pin an old brooch to a plain hat.
- Use an antique silk scarf as a shawl and secure it with an antique brooch.
- Antique boas are a fun way to dress up an outfit.

What are some of the things to look for and beware of when buying vintage clothes? Following are some general rules on buying antique clothing and wearable collectibles.

- Try it on. What appears to be a lot of fabric often has a specific fit; many of these clothes were tailor-made. Also, don't go by sizes; people in general were smaller proportioned in the past, and vintage sizes often don't match up with today's sizes.
- If you need to make alterations, make sure you can: Look for plenty of hem and sideseam fabric.
- Make sure the fabric is not too delicate to sew or clean—ask the store owner if it has been cleaned. Take the garment to a dry cleaner to find the best way to clean it. Examine it in the light for stains or discolorations; stains under the arms may be impossible to get rid of.
- Inspect the garment closely for tears. Tears of the hem or seams can generally be fixed without showing; a repaired rip in the fabric itself is tougher to conceal.
- Check to make sure any zippers are in good working order.
- Inspect the lining of a jacket. It can often cost more to replace an old lining than what you pay for the jacket itself.
- Above all, make sure it is comfortable.
- Don't forget to check antiques stores. These shops often carry an eclectic array of vintage clothing, from embroidered shawls and beaded purses to fur stoles and felt fedoras.

Sew Easy

The following tips come from Butterick Patterns design director Cheryl Coleman, a real-size customer herself and an avid home sewer. Sewing your own clothes allows you to shape a pattern to your own, specific proportions—and offers you a range of options that may not be available to you in retail stores in your community.

1. Any new fashion trend that comes out in misses' sizes works equally well for real-size women with only slight modifications.

2. When it comes to colors and fabrics, there are no hard-and-fast rules. If a fabric you like is suitable for a garment, then use it. Fashion statements are not made just in colors but in textures as well—suedes, leathers, corduroys, and knits are great choices for the real-size woman. Invest in soft fabrics such as silk or rayon blends for easy draping.

3. Garment lengths are a personal issue. If you have great legs, show them. Generally, altering your skirts to mid-knee or two inches below midknee is a very flattering length.

4. When it comes to pants, if you like to wear very narrow widths such as fourteen inches or smaller, you must balance the top with longer tunics or jackets. The top garment should fall between below hip to midthigh.

5. You can soften a dull classic blazer career look by making a cardigan or shirt jacket instead to go with your suit bottoms. Shirt jackets give your outfit a feminine, contemporary look. A vest is also a great alternative to a jacket, giving you a polished, updated look.

6. Select home sewing patterns that have V necks, which produce a long, slimming look.

7. The best looks in jackets cover your hips or are longer. Adjust the pieces to your body type when using home sewing patterns.

8. Like scarves but feel you have no neck? No problem. Long, flowing scarves draped loosely around the neck

look pretty and feminine. You can make a long, sheer scarf that will complement any outfit.

9. If you are 5'4" or shorter, you are a petite. Because fashionable clothing for petite plus sizes is hard to find, making your own outfits is often the best way to build a wardrobe. With petite-adjusted patterns you can address fit and proportion problems and fashion a perfect-fitting garment.

10. Comfort is key. If your clothing is too long, too short, too loose, or too binding, you simply won't wear it.

Shopping for Bargains

Even though I know a little something about spending money, I do get a kick out of a great deal. Following are some shopping destinations that contain real bargains, as well as smart advice on how to find them.

Thrift Shops

You know how some people can walk into a shop crammed with merchandise and like a divining rod head straight for a real gem? That's called having a nose for value. Many shoppers have the gift of uncovering treasure at thrift shops, while others take home fool's gold. Goodwill and Salvation Army stores have a huge variety of items, and you need plenty of time to sift through them. A better place to find bargains may be at community or church thrift shops, which are fund-raising vehicles run by folks who are offering goods at rock-bottom prices and are willing to haggle. I found some Victorian goblets at a church thrift shop for 50 cents each last year and a pair of 1940s leather driving gloves for $1.

Outlets

Keep in mind that many designers produce lower-quality clothes just for the outlet trade, so you may not be getting such a bargain after all. Also be sure to first check the prices in retail stores to make sure the outlets are giving you a bargain. Search out the "irregulars" bin, where garments with slight imperfections are sold for dirt-cheap prices. Go straight to the back of the stores where marked-down merchandise is put at season's end—that's where the real savings are. Save your outlet shopping for big holiday weekends, when discounted clothes are traditionally even more deeply discounted.

Consignment Shops

Here gently used clothing is brought in by private owners to sell, and the shop owner and the garment owner usually split the selling price. Plus-size consignment shops are popping up all over the country; look in your Yellow Pages for one near you. Consignment shops are a great way to get a quality piece of clothing at a low price—plus you can try the garment on before you buy. One of the most popular items at consignment shops: bridal gowns. Bridal gowns at consignment shops are generally in great condition—they've been worn only once.

Mac and I shared an off-camera moment during the filming of Love and Curses and All That Jazz in New Orleans.

Collection of Delta Burke

Mardi Gras Beads!
Collection of Delta Burke

One of our many Mardi Gras, with Mother and Uncle Jim.   Collection of Delta Burke

He's gorgeous and a great guy: Robert Urich and me in my <u>Delta</u> blond hair.

Collection of Delta Burke

DELTA BURKE

Our town: on the streets of New Orleans.
Collection of Delta Burke

Mac and I love to stay at the old plantations along the Mississippi. At Nottaway Plantation, we sneaked into this ballroom at night after the tours were over and danced by ourselves in our bare feet.

Collection of Delta Burke

Mac on one of our many road trips.
Collection of Delta Burke

Road trip: Florida girls have no business ice-skating.
Collection of Delta Burke

Mama Jean getting her daily exercise with Loretta in New Orleans.
Collection of Delta Burke

Blanche's birthday party. As the family cakemaker, I baked the cake. From left, that's Scarlett, Stella, Lucy, Blanche, and Loretta.
Collection of Delta Burke

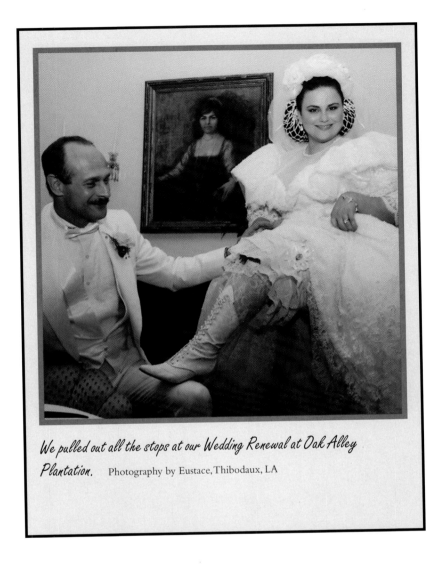

We pulled out all the stops at our Wedding Renewal at Oak Alley Plantation.   Photography by Eustace, Thibodaux, LA

We didn't know that this would be Nana and Blanche's last birthday party. Nana turned eighty-five on December 23, 1996. Full of spunk and character, she was a pistol. Collection of Delta Burke

"I never heard him say an unkind word about anyone," my mother says about
Dad, who passed away in 1984. He started the tradition of birthday bows on
the forehead. Continuing the legacy (above), Mom, Jennifer, and Nana
wear bows at Nana's last birthday.   Photos collection of Delta Burke

On the set of Mac's TV drama <u>Promised Land</u> in 1996, with Celeste Holm and Marian Ross.

Collection of Delta Burke

In my role as Melanie Darrow, a crime-fighting lawyer, on the USA network.

Photofest (*Melanie Darrow*). Brian Smith

Mom and me at her birthday party at Dunleith Plantation.
Collection of Delta Burke

My wonderful, supportive Mac here on Valentine's Day in Los Angeles.
Collection of Delta Burke

Delta Style: Blanche, Scarlett, and Stella (in tiara), living the good life with a portrait of me (by Colleen Ross) as backdrop.
Collection of Delta Burke

CHAPTER 7

The Story So Far

New Orleans:
Where the Heart Is

The first time I saw New Orleans, I was doing a TV movie called *Johnny Blue* with Gil Gerard. I had Mother come up, and we toured River Road, lined with big white plantations and live oaks dripping with Spanish moss. In New Orleans, I discovered Mardi Gras beads. I love Mardi Gras, but I *really* love Mardi Gras beads. I've had guys dragging Hefty garbage bags of ten-cent beads down the street for me.

Being from the South is a strong bond for Mac and me. Mac is even more rooted there than I am. He was born and raised in Mississippi and worked in the Louisiana oil fields and the offshore rigs for years so that he could feed his family and do theater work. His ties to the land, his family, his kids Jessica, Angus, and Katie, and old friends have kept him grounded. Mac put it best when he said he felt like he'd been on location in Los Angeles for sixteen years. His home is down South, and I feel the same way.

So we started looking for a Southern base with a real sense of place. When I was in therapy, I did a lot of writing in my journal about my needs and desires. At the time, I was concerned with living in a place where I could walk around and not be watched all the time, not feel there were always cameras or eyes on me, always judging. Another thing I explored in my diaries was getting to the heart of what made me happy. I immediately thought of the peace I felt daydreaming in a chair beside my grandmother's lake, the honeysuckle scent that would sneak into an open window in summer, and the thrill of seeing big white egrets swoop down to touch the earth. I missed the rhythm of the South's sunny, easy pace.

Mac and I had both fallen in love with the city of New Orleans when Mac directed *Love and Curses and All that Jazz*. It was big-time Southern, it was colorful and quirky, it had history and culture, and yet it had a small-town feel. We decided to pull out of the Hollywood rat race and make New Orleans our permanent base—and try to get a semblance of normalcy in our lives.

So in August 1995, we moved. It took something like eight moving vans to haul the Burke/McRaney collection from the West Coast to our new homes—a house in New Orleans and a five-hundred-acre farm in Mississippi. Mac and I drove cross-country in his green Suburban with stuff piled up all around us. Because we were carrying all the valuable things—the diaries, the jewelry—we felt uncomfortable leaving the car exposed whenever we stopped at a motel for the night. So I'd strut into a nice cozy motel room with the five dogs in tow and leave Mac to sleep in the car. I needed a good night's sleep after spending a day riding with the country's number-one law-abiding citizen. Mac always drives just *under* the speed limit and *will not* pass a car without putting on his signals— before he passes, while he passes, after he passes. Doesn't matter if it's a two-lane, four-lane, or ten-lane road or if the car we're planning to pass is a mile up the road. On go the signals. All the way through Arizona. *Click-click. Click-click.* New Mexico. *Click-click. Click-click.* Texas. *Click-click. Click-click.*

We even hauled some of our favorite bushes and trees from the yard in Pasadena to the farm. Certain plants had sentimental value and I just couldn't leave them, like a favorite hydrangea bush that reminded me of Nana. We planted it at the farm, and it's doing great. Remember that white rosebush Mac and I planted on our wedding eve in Los Angeles? It now resides in a prominent spot at the farm. An air plant that Nana and I had in Los Angeles—which was attached to a piece of

Scarlett, Stella, and Blanche were not happy campers on our canoe trip. Here they are giving me that "put-upon" look. Collection of Delta Burke

driftwood she found on the beach—traveled to Pasadena and finally to the farm. A little-bitty cactus Nana and I bought at the L.A. farmers' market has traveled with me from house to house, getting bigger and bigger each step of the way. In fact, I've attached a sort of symbolism to that plant. After all these years, it's still sprouting, still growing—and I'm doing the same.

In New Orleans, we found an old Creole townhouse with a big courtyard in back and ceilings up to here. Our dogs Scarlett, Bitsy, Loretta, and Lucy have the run of the place. They also like to dabble in show biz every now and then. My beautiful Blanche, who had been with me from my early days in Hollywood, died last year. She was a real ham; she made an appearance on *Hollywood Squares* back in 1986. To add to this menagerie is a snow-white cockatoo named Lily, a bird forever frozen in the mentality of a three-year-old child. She drinks my coffee, eats my food, and loves to take showers—anything I like, she likes.

Mac's family lives close by in Mississippi. Our farm is just a couple of hours' drive from New Orleans. It's a working farm, with watermelons being the main crop. I usually have a big garden and get out there and plant seeds in my bare feet. When we're both home, we hit the road as "White Trash on Wheels"—taking B&B road trips with discarded candy and junk-food wrappers littering the car floor. We like to stay at the old plantation inns and spend our evenings watching riverboats coil around the bends in the Mississippi.

Not long ago we celebrated with a marriage "renewal" at Oak Alley Plantation in Louisiana, a big Southern-style party where Mac wore a white suit and hat and rode down the oak allée on a white horse. I made a grand entrance in a horse and carriage. It was so much fun we decided to renew our vows on a regular basis.

Better still, I convinced my mother and my sister, Jennifer, to move to New Orleans. My beloved grandmother Nana passed away here last year. Recently my brother, Jonathan,

Lily at the farm—in the swamp, actually. Maybe that's why she has such a startled look on her face. Collection of Delta Burke

Mac and I love to take road trips. We saw this pond and decided to get our feet wet. Just a couple of hicks at heart. Collection of Delta Burke

decided to move here. My family lives just a few blocks away, and we talk to or visit each other just about every day. When I'm in town, I take painting lessons from Melissa Neff, an artist who has a studio in a little garret in the Quarter. Way up above the city, the French doors open up to the river breeze and the Vieux Carré rooftops gleam in the sun. It's such a contrast to California, where moving about is a big production. Here, I'm free and happy. I walk through the old town and poke my head into little shops. I go to art galleries and gossip with my neighbors. Everyone you meet is an artist or a writer or a professor at Ole Miss or a Pulitzer Prize–winner. It's an interesting mix of people, eclectic and odd. And even though I'm on location part of the time, in New Orleans I've got a real home to return to. And a solid sense of place reinforces a sense of self, I've found. I've come home in more ways than one.

That Thing About Weight

My weight will always be an issue. I know that I will never be a size 6 again, nor do I want to make the unhappy sacrifices to do so. I thought that being thin would make me happy. It never did. Nowadays I find that my weight stays at a healthy level and even goes down naturally when I'm busy doing something I love. Oh, I'm still curvy and bosomy—and always will be. But feeling good about myself and the weight I'm at now means dealing with the sexual power again. It will be interesting to see how I handle it. I hope I can draw on my newfound strength to be comfortable and confident with the sexual power.

Streetcar Named Desire

My life has undergone plenty of change. I achieved a sort of celebrity early on, which allowed me to collect lots of "stuff."

But when I moved out of L.A., I let go of the big life. That wasn't easy, believe me. Leaving our house in Los Angeles, our fantasy movie star house, wasn't easy either. But it was also what I called a "two-sitcom house"—and when you're working so hard to pay for it and you're never there, what is the point? Oh, I liked the trappings of fame—they were hard to let go of. But most of it wasn't real. And in the process I let go of that lifestyle and all that went with it, including a way of thinking.

I always said I wanted to die on stage an old woman, and in very dramatic fashion. But I suddenly reached a point where I thought, Maybe there is something else I want to do in life, maybe this isn't it. That really threw me. But I decided to embrace change and try going off in directions I didn't intend to go. Maybe I'll find the way I was supposed to go all along.

❝ *I think the remarkable thing is not so much that the whole ordeal made her tougher, but that she emerged with her sensitivity to others intact. And I think that's the trick. She's just as optimistic about things as she used to be. And you know what? After the weight gain, Delta started doing her best work; it made her a better actress.* ❞ —Gerald McRaney

It's rare for an actress to have the opportunity to play more than one smart, sexy, sassy woman in one lifetime. My latest incarnation, Melanie Darrow, a lawyer who solves crimes on the side, is another strong, funny female role. In 1991, I did *Love Letters* on stage in Los Angeles with Mac, and doing theater work made me feel like a real actress again. For a switch, I had a dramatic role in the 1996 CBS TV movie *A Promise to Carolyn,* which had what I thought was one of the best scripts I've read in years. I was apprehensive about doing drama after having done comedy for so long. I realized I'm not as bold as I was when I first hit Hollywood and thought I could do everything.

Shooting photographs from the waist up for Delta Burke Design. Louis Sahuc

❝ *Delta is easily one of the top five comediennes in the business today. She has great timing and a great ear. Her read on things is like no one else's. She knows the melody of comedy. It would be a crime for her not to continue to do comedy; she's simply so good at it.* ❞ —Linda Bloodworth-Thomason

Another side of me, Delta Burke, actress and show-biz ham, loves to play the gracious star. Then there's my design work for Delta Burke Design, which is extremely fulfilling. When I'm home, I'm painting in my studio or taking photography classes or catching up with my friends, the fascinating people of the Quarter. Mac and I have been cooking up something else. We get a kick out of helping young or undiscovered artists and actors get started, connecting them up with others. We'd like to find a bigger way to do that. Mac loves teaching, so maybe in our old age we'll become schoolmarms.

I recently visited the site of my old home in Florida. All the old familiar talismans are there—the mulberry trees that dyed my feet purple when I climbed them, the magnolias, the orange groves—but now they share space with a four-lane highway. My house is gone. All that's left is a scattering of bricks from the old driveway. (Of course, I filched a couple as keepsakes.) I keep searching for a place like that, with the smell of the earth and the closeness to nature. Oh, I love New Orleans, but my house there will *not* be my last house. I'll keep looking for that simple farmhouse and the magical life I led there.

And while I do, I'll be busy reveling in the woman I've become. I have time to meander down the sweet little roads of backcountry America, seeing places and people I never would have seen if I hadn't got off the freeway. I can give my full attention to developing my craft. All the things I put on hold more than twenty years ago. I've got a lot of living to do yet—this time, from the inside out. I'll keep you informed.

CHAPTER 8

Real-Size Resource Guide

When I went to London to study acting in the 1970s, the city's flea markets, bazaars, and boutiques were in their heyday. Today I live in another shopper's paradise. In New Orleans I find things I see nowhere else on earth, and even if I don't buy anything, I'm always inspired. If I have any real advice, it's to *shop creatively*. Why *not* look in vintage shops for roomy men's jackets? Why not use an old dress to cover a footstool? Why not turn buttons into earrings? Or hats into wall hangings?

Don't forget the power of the consumer. If you feel you haven't gotten your money's worth when buying a service, make your unhappiness known. And if you think a product or service should be offered, and it's not, go to your sources and ask for it.

Here are some places to find the things you need.

My Favorite New Orleans Shops

Shopping in New Orleans is as much fun as eating gumbo and listening to jazz. I always find something new or surprising when I meander around the city—and believe me, I can do a lot of damage in just a few short blocks. My favorite hangouts are art galleries, bookstores, and antiques shops, where I ogle not only the home furnishings but the luscious vintage jewelry. Below is a sampling of my favorite shops; if I've left anybody out, I sincerely apologize. Maybe I just haven't gotten to you yet! Have fun—and tell 'em Delta sent you.

GRACE NOTE. *Fabulous, romantic store that features quality vintage and new clothing, antique textiles and accessories, and handmade hats (900 Royal Street; 504-522-1513; RXR13@aol.com).*

THE SHOP OF TWO SISTERS. *Beautiful and unique collectibles, clothes, and home furnishings (838 Royal Street; 504-524-6213).*

FLEUR DE PARIS. *Ultraromantic dresses in imported fabrics and couture construction, and custom millinery straight out of Victorian times (712 Royal Street; 504-525-1899).*

HAROLD CLARKE COUTURIER ATELIER. *Former New York designer Harold Clarke makes couture costumes and gowns (1528 Jackson Avenue; 504-522-0777).*

LAZYBUG. *Collectibles and clothes made by local artisans include hand-painted glassware and great jackets (600 Royal Street; 504-524-3649; Riverwalk: 504-525-1301).*

THE LIVING ROOM. *Fun, unusual crafts and housewares with a nod to local history; includes lamps made with ceramic pieces from eighteenth-century privies and picture frames fashioned from 150-year-old cypress plantation structures (927 Royal Street; 504-595-8860).*

PELIGRO. *Big, colorful art gallery featuring the work of local artists like the delightful Glitter Girl, and self-taught favorite sons such as Big Al the shoeshine man (305 Decatur Street; 504-581-1706).*

THREE-DOG BAKERY. *Food shop for dogs. Treat your pet to a gourmet snack or hold its birthday party right there in the store (827 Royal Street; 504-525-2253; fax: 504-525-2252).*

NEW ORLEANS HAT COMPANY. *Mac and I love to buy our hats here (402 Chartres Street; 504-524-8794).*

LIBRAIRIE BOOKSHOP. *Musty old French Quarter bookstore with lots of ambience and hard-to-find books (823 Chartres Street; 504-525-4837).*

BODY HANGINGS. *Capes, cloaks, and shawls (835 Decatur Street; 800-574-1823 or 504-524-9856).*

QUILT SHOP IN NEW ORLEANS. *Quilts, for making or buying (816 Decatur Street; 504-522-0835).*

OH SUSANNAH. *Beautiful collector dolls (518 St. Peter Street; 504-586-8701).*

GINJA JAR AND GINJA JAR TOO. *Art collectibles such as hand-made Mardi Gras masks (607 Royal Street; 800-259-7643 or 504-523-7614).*

FAULKNER HOUSE BOOKS. *Bookstore in house where William Faulkner lived in the 1920s (624 Pirate's Alley; 504-524-2940).*

A GALLERY OF FINE PHOTOGRAPHY. *Rare and museum-quality photos and books (322 Royal Street; 504-568-1313).*

BERGEN GALLERIES. *Owned by colorful local favorite Margarita Bergen (730 Royal Street; 800-621-6179 or 504-523-7882).*

DYANSEN GALLERY *(433 Royal Street; 504-523-2902).*

HANSON GALLERY—NEW ORLEANS INC. *(229 Royal Street; 504-524-8211).*

SUTTON GALLERIES *(519 Royal Street; 504-581-6925).*

DIXON AND DIXON *(237 Royal Street; 504-524-0282).*

KIELS ANTIQUES. *Antique furnishings and objets d'art (325 Royal Street; 504-522-4552).*

M. S. RAU. *Antique furniture, glass, china, silver (630 Royal Street; 800-544-9440 or 504-523-5660).*

MOSS ANTIQUES. *French and English antiques and estate jewelry (411 Royal Street; 504-522-3981).*

ROYAL ANTIQUES *(307–309 Royal Street; 504-524-7033).*

Nationwide Retail Department Stores

DILLARDS. *Retail department stores (call 501-376-5200 for store locations).*

J. C. PENNEY. *Retail department stores (call 800-222-6161 for store locations).*

CATHERINE'S. *Retail department stores (call 901-398-9500 for store locations).*

MERCANTILE STORES. *Retail department stores (call 513-881-8000 for the exact locations and telephone numbers of the stores listed below).*

Maison Blanche (New Orleans, Louisiana).

Joslins (*Englewood, Colorado*).

J. B. White (*Augusta, Georgia, and Columbia, South Carolina*).

Castner Knott (*Nashville, Tennessee*).

McAlpine's (*Lexington, Kentucky*).

Bacon's (*Louisville, Kentucky*).

Jones Stores (*Kansas City, Missouri*).

VON MAUR. *Retail department stores (call 319-388-2200 for store locations).*

MACY'S EAST. *Retail department stores (call 212-695-4400 for store locations).*

SAKS FIFTH AVENUE. *Retail department stores (call 800-345-3454 for store locations).*

LORD & TAYLOR. *Retail department stores (call 800-223-7440 for store locations).*

On-Line Shop

REAL BODIES: CLOTHING FROM BALI. *Mail-order and on-line clothing company selling women's apparel in island-style batik and print patterns made by Balinese artisans in all sizes (for catalog, send $2 to Real Bodies, 663 Falmouth, Massachusetts 02540-3215; phone: 508-548-5260; fax: 508-548-7701; Web site: contact@ realbodies.com).*

Shoes/Belts

SELBY'S. *Carries a variety of hard-to-fit sizes, especially for the wide foot.*

MASSEY'S. *Mail-order shoes for wide feet (catalog: 800-462-7739).*

SHOEXPRESS. *Mail-order shoes in large sizes (phone: 800-874-0469; Web site: www.shoexpress.com).*

THE CUSTOM FOOT. *Custom-made shoes (call 800-440-8814 for store locations).*

LORI ALEXANDRE. *Wide-calf boots in sizes 5 to 13 and calf sizes 16 inches to 24 inches (7999 Boul Les Gal. #N012, Anjou, Quebec H1M-1W6 Canada; 800-648-4735; 514-355-8500).*

H. L. S. BELTS. *Plus-size belts in sizes 3X/48–5" waist (4757 West Park #106, Suite 410, Plano, Texas 75093; 214-985-0074).*

Maternity Clothes

J. C. PENNEY *(catalog: 800-222-6161).*

BOSOM BUDDIES. *Nursing bras to sizes 46I and maternity clothes (P.O. Box 6138, Kingston, New York 12401; 914-338-2038).*

BASICS DIRECT *(catalog: 800-954-6667).*

BETSY & CO. *(catalog: 800-77-BETSY).*

ABOVE AND BEYOND *(brochure: 800-285-4884).*

Hosiery and Underwear

GODDESS BRAS. *Wide selection, from comfortable all-cotton bras with no underwire to sexy push-ups and nursing bras (213-629-2905 or 617-569-3000).*

SILVER LINING. *On-line hosiery boutique offering sizes 14–26 (toll-free phone: 888-237-8385; fax: 404-237-8385; Web site: silverliningplus.com).*

JUST MY SIZE. *Hosiery, underwear, and bodywear for real sizes* (*catalog: 800-IT-FITS-ME*).

THE BUST SHOP. *Bras of all kinds—sports, maternity, strapless—for sizes 26A to 60-OO (8270 East 71 Street, Tulsa, Oklahoma 74133; 800-858-3887).*

HANES/L'EGGS/BALI/PLAYTEX. *Discounted hosiery and bras (800-300-2600).*

FREDERICK'S OF HOLLYWOOD. *Sexy, exotic lingerie to sizes 3X (800-323-9525).*

HIGH PLACES. *Victorian-style corsets and bustiers in sizes 18 to 26 (303-973-3412).*

NADINA PLUS. *Lingerie in natural fibers from sizes 12 to 32 (1124 Lonsdale Avenue #1176, Vancouver, British Columbia V7M-3J5 Canada; 604-985-2356).*

SWEET DREAMS INTIMATES. *Custom-made bras and foundations in unlimited sizes (81 Route 111, Smithtown, New York 11787; 516-366-0565).*

YELLOW CREEK DESIGNS. *Lingerie made to order in plus and super sizes (2901 Yellow Creek Road, Dickson, Tennessee 37055; 615-763-6147).*

Bridal Gowns

BIG, BEAUTIFUL BRIDES. *Order by mail (Toronto, Ontario Canada; 416-923-4673).*

LARGE AND LOVELY BRIDAL CENTER. *Bridal gowns and mother-of-the-bride wear in sizes 18 to 44+ (381 Sunrise Highway, Lynbrook, New York 11563; 516-599-7100).*

SEWING FASHION COUNCIL. *Offers tips on sewing your own wedding gown with Wedding Belles brochure. Simply send a $2 check* *payable to the American Home Sewing & Craft Association to Sewing Fashion Council, P.O. Box 650, Madison Square Station, New York, New York 10159-0650.*

Sewing Sources

FASHION FIT PATTERN SERVICE. *Will create custom-fit patterns on-line (www.finhost.fi/fashion/fashion/htm).*

Catalogs

LANE BRYANT. *Real-size clothing offered exclusively (800-477-7070).*

ROMAN'S. *Real-size clothing offered exclusively (800-274-7240).*

JUST MY SIZE. *Real-size clothing offered exclusively (800-522-0889). Also outlet stores (call 800-831-7489 for store locations).*

SPIEGEL'S FOR YOU CATALOG. *Caters to large-size women only (catalog: 800-345-4500).*

AMPLE STUFF. *Useful tools and things that make the lives of real-size people more comfortable (call for catalog or Ample Shopper's Newsletter: 914-679-3316).*

SILHOUETTES. *Comfortable, affordable styles in sizes 14 to 26 (800-704-3322).*

ULLA POPKEN. *European-styled clothing in plus sizes 12 to 30 (800-245-8552).*

LANDS' END. *Sporty clothing and swimsuits to size 20 (800-356-4444).*

MAKING IT BIG. *Natural-fiber clothing in sizes 14 to 44 (707-778-8988).*

THE RIGHT TOUCH. *Accessories, such as belts, scarves, jewelry, and hats, in bigger and longer proportions (800-233-2883).*

J. C. PENNEY. *Real-size clothing (catalog: 800-222-6161).*

Consignment Shops

FASHION FINDERY. *Full-figured consignment shop for sizes 14W and up (1660 Lane Avenue South, Jacksonville, Florida 32210; phone: 800-783-9888; Web site: www.jaxadnet.com/Fashion/).*

AMPLE ANNIE. *Retail and consignment (717 Pacific Avenue, Santa Cruz, California 95060; 408-425-3838).*

FAIRY GODMOTHER AT LARGE. *Retail and consignment (133 South Murphy Avenue, Sunnyvale, California 94086; 408-737-7684).*

Vintage Stores and Sources

THE INTERNET ANTIQUE SHOP. *On-line shop with photo gallery of such items as antique bakelite, pearl, or abalone buttons (antiques@tias.com).*

ALICE UNDERGROUND. *Pioneering retail store with wide range of quality vintage clothing (380 Columbus Avenue, New York, New York 10024; 212-724-6682).*

CUTTER'S RESEARCH JOURNAL. *A quarterly journal, put out by the United States Institute for Theatre Technology, Inc., that has original patterns and drafting instructions for period clothing and costumes (for subscriptions, contact Cutter's Research Journal, USITT, 6443 Ridings Road, Syracuse, New York 13206; phone: 800-93-USITT or 315-463-6463; Web site: www.ffa.ucalgary.ca/usitt/crj.html).*

Fabulous Flea Markets

THE GARAGE *(112 West 25th Street, New York, New York 10001; 212-243-5343).*

THE NEW 26TH ST. INDOOR ANTIQUES FAIR. *Indoor-outdoor Saturday and Sunday flea market with great deals on used and antique furniture, knickknacks, clothes, jewelry (122 West 26th Street, New York, New York 10001; 212-633-6010).*

Magazines

MODE. *An upscale look at real-size fashion (212-328-0180).*

BBW. *Consumer magazine that features comprehensive fashion, style, inspiration, and health tips for plus-size women (800-707-5592). BBW ONLINE updates articles and events monthly, offers shopping resources, and has quarterly on-line fashion shows (www2.bbwonline.com/bbwonline/).*

BELLE. *Magazine catering to African-American real-size women (800-877-5549).*

RADIANCE: THE MAGAZINE FOR LARGE WOMEN. *A consumer magazine for plus-size women (phone:510-482-0680; Web site: www.radiancemagazine.com.)*

Haircuts

Where can you pay $10 for a $100 haircut or $15 for a $200 color processing at a top salon? In cities all over the country, on discount nights. This is when stylists-in-training practice on real-life models—that is, anyone who calls up and makes an appointment for training night. For these salon apprentices, the haircut is an exam and as such will be scrutinized and graded by top stylists. For this reason, the haircut and appraisal may take more time than a typical haircut. You must call ahead for an appointment.

NEW YORK:

Oribe Salon (691 Fifth Avenue; 212-319-3910; call Tuesday mornings for evening appointment as hair model).

John Sahag Salon (425 Madison Avenue, 2nd floor; 212-750-7772; call for appointment as hair model).

Bumble & Bumble (146 East 56 Street; 212-521-6500; call for appointment as hair model).

Louis Licari Color Group, Inc. (797 Madison Avenue; 212-517-8084; call for appointment as hair model).

CHICAGO:

Michael Anthony Hair Salon & Aveda Day Spa (1001 West North Avenue; 312-649-0707; call for appointment as hair model).

Charles Ifergen (106 East Oak Street; 312-642-4484; call for appointment as hair model).

BEVERLY HILLS:

Jose Eber Salon (224 North Rodeo Drive; 310-278-7646; call for appointment as hair model).

ATLANTA:

Van Michael Salon and New Talents Salon (39 West Paces Ferry Road; 404-239-0320; call for appointment as hair model).

Skin Care Products

Alpha-hydroxy creams are sold through local dermatologists; no prescription needed. Recommended brands sold nationwide are MD FORTÉ (800-253-9499) and NEOSTRATA (800-852-7696). Call to find where these products are offered in your community.

Travel

RADIANCE TOURS. *Travel with other real-size women on specially tailored trips all over the world. Radiance Tours are a program of* Radiance: The Magazine for Large Women *and are organized to make travel comfortable and fun for large women. Some of the previous destination sites have been Maui, an Alaskan cruise, and a Caribbean cruise. Contact* Radiance: The Magazine for Large Women *(P.O. Box 30246, Oakland, California 94604; phone/fax: 510-482-0680).*

FANNY PACK. *Nylon pack for real-size people; custom-fit to your measurements (Ample Stuff; P.O. Box 116; Bearsville, New York 12409; for a catalog or order, phone: 914-679-3316; fax: 914-679-1206).*

SEAT-BELT EXTENDERS. *On your next flight on an airplane, take along your own seat-belt extender (Ample Stuff; phone: 914-679-3316; fax: 914-679-1206).*

Books

FAT CHANCE *by Leslea Newman. An award-winning story of a thirteen-year-old girl who thinks she's too heavy and who learns about bulimia from her slim best friend (New York: Putnam, 1994; $15.95).*

OUTLET BOUND: GUIDE TO THE NATION'S BEST OUTLETS. *Guide to outlet stores (800-336-8853; $7.95).*

WISE WOMEN DON'T WORRY, WISE WOMEN DON'T SING THE BLUES *by Jane Claypool. A down-to-earth guide of practical wisdom for women (Encinitas, California: Cornucopia Press, 1994; phone/fax: 619-942-1628; $11.95).*

WOMEN WHO RUN WITH THE WOLVES *by Clarissa Pinkola Estés, Ph.D. Best-seller on ancient myths and stories of women in the* *wild accompanied by sage advice and lessons for contemporary women out of touch with their instincts (New York: Ballantine Books, 1992; $15).*

SELF-ESTEEM COMES IN ALL SIZES *by Carol A. Johnson. How to boost your self-esteem (New York: Doubleday, 1995; $10.95).*

WHEN WOMEN STOP HATING THEIR BODIES *by Jane R. Hirschmann and Carol H. Munter. Learning to accept yourself (New York: Fawcett, 1995; $12).*

Social Groups and Self-Help Organizations

NATIONAL ASSOCIATION TO ADVANCE FAT ACCEPTANCE (NAAFA). *Human-rights organization involved on social, legal, and educational fronts to promote acceptance and end discrimination for large people. You can contact NAAFA to locate chapters and social groups in your state or community, find out how to join, or order books, brochures, or videos (P.O. Box 188620, Sacramento, California 95818; 800-442-1214; talk to a staff member at 916-558-6880, Monday–Friday, 9–4; fax: 916-558-6881; Web site: www.naafa.org/).*

LARGESSE, THE NETWORK FOR SELF-ESTEEM. *Resource center with information and literature on organizations, legal rights, and self-help groups (P.O. Box 9404, New Haven, Connecticut 06534-0404; phone/fax: 203-787-1624; Web site: 75773.717@compuserve.com).*

LARGELY POSITIVE. *Self-help organization that promotes health and emotional well-being for real-size people (Glendale, Wisconsin; 414-454-6500).*

AMERICAN ANOREXIA/BULIMIA ASSOCIATION *(call 212-501-8351 for information, referrals, and help.)*

NATIONAL ASSOCIATION OF ANOREXIA NERVOSA AND ASSOCIATED DISORDERS *(call 708-831-3438 for referrals, support groups, and treatment information).*

Miscellaneous

+SIZE™ CHAIR. *Ergonomic office chairs for plus-size bottoms. From BioFit Engineered Seating (phone: 800-597-0246; fax: 419-823-1342).*

EXTRA-LONG TAPE MEASURE. *Heavy-duty 96-inch tape measure (Ample Stuff; P.O. Box 116, Bearsville, New York 12409; for a catalog or order, phone: 914-679-3316; fax: 914-679-1206).*

Resourceful Women: Style Tips from the Delta Burke Design Advisory Council

We asked members of the Delta Burke Design Advisory Council from all over the United States to contribute to the book with personal style or resource tips. We were overwhelmed by their generosity and enthusiasm—and good solid advice. From every corner of the country, their voices resonated with strength, pride, and confidence.

❝ *Look for swimwear that covers the hips with a skirt or wraparound.* ❞ —Terri Mullins, Nashville, Tennessee

❝ *I find it a good idea to put color swatches against my face in the light. It helps me see what the color accentuates. But I guess the best advice is to buy what you love, and you will look better in it because you will feel better in it.* ❞

—Louise Ahart, Marysville, California

❝ *I like high heels in large sizes. You don't have to go around all the time wearing pumps or flats! As for lingerie, you'd think most of the clothing manufacturers think we plus-size women all sleep in big T-shirts. But we like to look sexy too. In general, if you feel good in it and have the right attitude, you look good.* ❞

—Leslie Anderson, Everman, Texas

" *Accessories are important—but don't overaccessorize. You don't need to wear big, bulky jewelry. But I have one question to ask Delta: How about a cosmetics line, Delta?* **"**

—Patti Ann Hamilton, San Diego, California

" *Since I travel a lot on business, in different climates and events, I must pack intelligently, which requires more than 'throwing everything in a suitcase.' When traveling through warmer and colder places, for example, I select clothes that can be layered. Even my coat is a raincoat with a heavy liner, which works for rain and snow. The most important item is a cashmere cardigan of neutral color. For shoes, I pack one pair of comfortable black pumps, which can become dressy with shoe clips for the evening, one other pair of short/sturdy heels, and one pair of pretty sandals.* **"** —Edmea McCarty, Alexandria, Virginia

" *I am on a mailing list for a group called 'Large Encounters—for Large Women and the Men Who Love Them.' It is a dating service that I think other real-size women should know about. What I don't like about some of these large-size dating services, however, is that many men who advertise prefer extremely large women, to the point where these women are an unhealthy size. I happen to be overweight but not overly so, and I work out on a daily basis and am always conscious of staying healthy. So my advice to single women is to be wary of some of these advertisements.* **"** —Dina DiLucca, New York, New York

" *Feel good about yourself—that's what makes you look good. It's even more important than your clothes.* **"**

—Kenni Lynn Nicholson, Uniontown, Pennsylvania

❝ *I've got a list. Here it is:*

1. Avoid 'always,' 'never,' and 'only' when shopping. Explore and experiment; the tried and true may not be the best for you after all.
2. Invest in quality clothing, accessories, and cosmetics—you're worth it.
3. Avoid time traps and safety zones (example: if it's been more than a year since someone complimented your hairstyle, it may be time for a new look).
4. Learn to appreciate the difference between dressing up and dressing well.
5. If someone has a problem with your size, it's his or her problem.
6. The difference between good and great is attention to detail. A nice outfit can become a fabulous ensemble with the right shoes, jewelry, handbag, and so on. Select handbags and jewelry in proportions that are the most flattering for your shape and size. Pay attention to color, cut, fabrics, and hemlines when trying on clothes.
7. Find what truly makes you happy in life and live it! Happiness is sexy, secure, and contagious. Give it a try!**❞** —Lou Ann Woerner, Tallahassee, Florida

❝ *I like monotones, with something dark underneath and maybe a colorful jacket or vest over the top.* **❞**

—Mary Traverso, Asbury Park, New Jersey

❝ *In Alexandria, I'm a member of Made in Brazil (MIB), a small group of Brazilian-born women living permanently in the United States. We meet the first Monday of every month. Our clothing follows more along the lines of European styles. We* strive to dress in a feminine, classy way, no matter what our ages and sizes. We discuss what and where we shop for our clothes and accessories. 99 —Edmea McCarty, Alexandria, Virginia

66 I always buy a two-piece dress, a skirt with a jacket or top that comes over the skirt. When I wear pants and tops, I wear the tops that come down over your hips. 99

—Myrtil Pemberton, Wetumpka, Alabama

66 Like Delta, have a defiant nature! Be proud of who you are, whatever your size. 99 —Donna Black, Lexington, North Carolina

66 I am hard to please and hard to fit, and I am thrilled to death when I find someone like Delta who makes clothing that doesn't make me look like a circus clown. My advice is to avoid A-lines—they make you look twice as big as you are. Same with wide skirts—look for a tapered look instead. Find a soft fabric that flows down and hangs slim, and you're all right. Look for colors, but not big old red flowers or anything like that. 99 —Dorothy N. Williams, Bowling Green, Kentucky

66 Try it on! 99 —Val Walsh, Juneau, Alaska

66 The biggest mistake women make is trying to follow current fashion trends. Instead, decide what looks good on you—and what you're comfortable wearing. Don't worry about what's 'in.' Wear what looks good. 99 —Jean Evans, Ellicott City, Maryland

66 Don't wear clothes that are too short or too long. Always wear stockings that match your shoes. And skip those big flowers or plaids. 99 —Lila Barsky, Hillside, New Jersey

66 Some of these clothes for plus-size women are quite ugly— bag dresses, uncomplimentary materials. My advice is to spend

the money to find the right fitted clothes. Don't ever wear poorly fitted clothes. And don't be afraid to express yourself—don't hide yourself with dark, baggy outfits. Don't be afraid to wear brighter clothes—they make you look and feel happier. **99**

—Sandy Denhart, Columbus, Ohio

66 I'm a short large woman, and I find what works best is dressing in one color, without prints or flowers. I wear the same color top and bottom, so I'm not cutting myself off at the waist. Then I accessorize with pretty scarves, jewelry, or hats. **99**

—Tricia Young, Atherton, California

66 Use color to accentuate your positive aspects. I'm pear-shaped, so I wear dark on the bottom and color up toward my face. I pay a lot of attention to accessories. **99**

—Jackie Davis, Liberty, Missouri